High
Impact
Time
Management

High
Impact
Time
Management

William T. Brooks
and
Terry W. Mullins

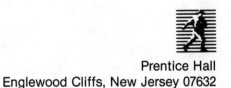

Prentice Hall
Englewood Cliffs, New Jersey 07632

Library of Congress Cataloging-in-Publication Data

Brooks, William T.
   High impact time management / by William T. Brooks and Terry W.
Mullins.
      p.   cm.
   Includes index.
   ISBN 0-13-387721-3
   1. Time management.   I. Mullins, Terry Wayne.   II. Title.
HD69.T54B76 1989
658.4'093--dc19   88-31618
                                                         CIP

Editorial/production supervision
  and interior design: Jacqueline A. Jeglinski
Cover design: Lundgren Graphics, Ltd.
Manufacturing buyer: Mary Ann Gloriande

 © 1989 by Prentice-Hall, Inc.
A division of Simon & Schuster
Englewood Cliffs, New Jersey 07632

The publisher offers discounts on this book when ordered
in bulk quantities. For more information, write:

> Special Sales/College Marketing
> Prentice-Hall, Inc.
> College Technical and Reference Division
> Englewood Cliffs, NJ 07632

Printed in the United States of America
10 9 8 7 6 5 4 3 2 1

ISBN 0-13-387721-3

Prentice-Hall International (UK) Limited, *London*
Prentice-Hall of Australia Pty. Limited, *Sydney*
Prentice-Hall Canada Inc., *Toronto*
Prentice-Hall Hispanoamericana, S.A., *Mexico*
Prentice-Hall of India Private Limited, *New Delhi*
Prentice-Hall of Japan, Inc., *Tokyo*
Simon & Schuster Pte. Ltd., *Singapore*
Editora Prentice-Hall do Brasil, Ltda., *Rio de Janeiro*

This book is dedicated to
Nancy Brooks and Paula Mullins
who have shared our struggles to become
better time managers.

Contents

PART II   ELIMINATING TIME WASTERS

PART III   REDUCING OTHER PEOPLE'S PRIORITIES

PART IV   GIVING UP FIRE FIGHTING

Preface

This book is for people with too much to do and too little time. Our challenge was to write a book that would help the reader to strike a balance between pursuit of ambition and building a fulfilling personal life. We offer hope for ambitious people who refuse to sacrifice everything else for their quest for success.

Effective time management can improve the quality of your life. You **can** accomplish more at work while building a richer personal life. High impact time management provides both the philosophical perspective and the nuts and bolts techniques required to get maximum benefit from each day.

The cause of most time management problems is the inability to link the hectic activities of a busy day to long–term priorities. When you fail to plan, your long-term goals are merely pipedreams. Unless your plans are translated into daily tasks, you become the victim of every tempest in a teapot. You find yourself responding to urgent demands that are of little importance to your long range goals or effectiveness.

High impact time management helps you break the habit of crisis management, the single most destructive management practice of poor time managers. You will learn to substitute goal setting, planning, scheduling, delegation, and follow-up for crisis management. Mastery of these skills enables you to increase the impact of the time you devote to work. High impact time management show you how to hold merely urgent tasks at bay while you complete important projects.

Mastery of these skills will not cure all of your time management problems. Life is difficult, and it is likely you will always have more things to do than you can possibly get done. However, high impact time management will provide you with the tools to make the task more manageable.

CHAPTER 1

Introduction: What Is High-Impact Time Management?

Everyone wants to manage time well. Many managers and other professionals make a conscious effort to manage time effectively. Paradoxically, few succeed.

Effective time management requires more than a "to do" list and good intentions. It is not enough to get up in the morning and solemnly pledge, "Today, yes, today, I'll do a better job of managing my time." Our approach to time management, called **high-impact time management**, requires three things:

1. An understanding of the value of time and where time goes
2. An understanding of the specific tools and skills of time management
3. Practice in using the tools and skills of time management

There are two key differences between high-impact time management and other approaches to time management. The first is a sympathetic recognition of where the time goes. The second is the use of our unique and copyrighted **Time Analysis Grid** for identifying your particular pattern of time use.

Figuring out where the time goes is an essential first step in improving your time management skills. When it comes to time management, most people feel that they are less effective than they intend to be. They are also bewildered that good-faith efforts do not seem to make much difference. This problem is particularly frustrating because it undermines one's self-esteem and self-confidence.

Two kinds of events consistently erode our best efforts to organize our time. First is unanticipated activity. Unexpected problems frequently distract us from our dutifully constructed "to do" lists. The second is other people's priorities. Throughout the workday you probably receive requests for assistance and cooperation from a variety of people both inside and outside your organization.

Some of these requests are quite justified and help you get your own work done while helping the person making the request. At other times, you are making a very large investment in someone else's priorities without a corresponding benefit to your own priorities. The trick is to distinguish between the two.

See if this example rings true. You arrive at work eager to get started on a carefully planned project, only to find an urgent message to call one of your best customers. You make the call and discover that the shipment promised for last Thursday still has not arrived. You start by calling Shipping, and three hours and six calls later you find out that the truck making the delivery is in a repair shop in Denver. By noon you have arranged for another trucking company to pick up the load and deliver it by 11:00 A.M. tomorrow.

As you start to pick up your **To Do List** to see if there is anything that can be salvaged before lunch, your phone rings. It is the Personnel Department wanting to know why you are a week late turning in the United Way contribution envelopes for your department. You have forgotten this little detail and promise to have it done before the day is over. After lunch, most of the afternoon is spent trying to track down people in your department to get their United Way envelopes back.

At 3:30 you are finally able to put some concentrated time into preparing the sales proposal that is due next Monday. Even this time is interrupted twice by the telephone and three times by people who stick their heads in your door and ask, "Do you have a minute?"

Notice that both unanticipated events and other people's priorities were involved in drawing attention away from the To Do List. At the beginning of the day, the To Do List represented the best estimate of what should be accomplished that day. The list was probably prepared based on an understanding of the importance and urgency of each of the tasks listed. Yet only a few hours later the day had been consumed with almost no time devoted to the items of the list. And that is where the time goes.

The **High-Impact Time Management System** shows you how to reduce the time devoted to other people's priorities. It also gives you a set of tools for preventing or at least doing a better job of managing unanticipated activities. The first tool for understanding where the time goes is the Time Analysis Grid. The Time Analysis Grid classifies activities in terms of their importance and the degree to which they are anticipated. (See Figure 1-1.)

The High-Impact Time Management System helps you to find more time to spend achieving your **targeted accomplishments** (cell 1 of the grid). Another significant boost in your overall effectiveness will come from meeting the challenges posed by **fire fighting** (cell 2 of the grid). Additional major gains in your ability to get control of your time will come from eliminating the need to spend time on **other people's priorities** (cell 3) and **time wasters** (cell 4).

COUNTDOWN TO ACCOMPLISHMENT

Increasing the time spent on planned accomplishments is the primary goal of the High-Impact Time Management System. However, we will not begin with cell 1 (targeted accomplishment) of the grid. We begin with cell 4 (time wasters) and countdown through cell 3 (other people's priorities) and cell 2 (fire fighting) to reach cell 1 (targeted accomplishment). The topics are dealt with in this order for a reason. Time becomes available for targeted accomplishments only when you have learned to eliminate time wasters, to resist other people's priorities, and to organize to avoid fighting fires.

Time wasters come in many forms. They include telephone interruptions, drop-in visitors, procrastination, waiting for

	Anticipated Activity	Unanticipated Activity
Important	1 Targeted Accomplishment	2 Fire Fighting
Unimportant	3 Other People's Priorities	4 Time Wasters

Figure 1-1   Time Analysis Grid

meetings to start, hopping from project to project, and doing low-priority things simply because they are easy or pleasant. They also include hunting for things because you are disorganized, are doing paperwork that should be delegated, and attending unnecessary meetings. The chapter devoted to dealing with time wasters (Chapter 4) will show you how to reduce time wasters to a bare minimum.

Other people's priorities present a dilemma. On the one hand, cooperation and teamwork are the hallmarks of effective management and corporate etiquette. On the other hand, helping others to achieve their priorities at the sacrifice of your own goals is foolish. The chapters devoted to controlling the demands others place on you will provide guidelines for appropriate cooperation.

Learning to manage your activities effectively enough to avoid the need to spend your time fighting fires is a significant challenge. For many of us, just learning to live without fighting fires will mean breaking lifelong habits. However, our chapters on problem solving, decision making, and delegation provide most of the tools necessary to prevent crisis management. Mastery of these skills sets the stage for real achievement.

Targeted accomplishment results from establishing priorities, setting goals, identifying milestones, and meeting deadlines. The High-Impact Time Management System shows you how to devote the major portion of your workday to planned activities of high importance. It also allows you to link your daily To Do List to your major career goals.

HOW TO ANALYZE YOUR TIME

Your first step to better time management is a clear picture of how you currently use your time. The next several pages are devoted to your personal **Time-Use Log.** Use the log to record your time use over the next seven days. You may be tempted to ignore this request because you conscientiously make To Do Lists and feel you know where your time goes. Nevertheless, this exercise is critical.

Most people think of their use of time in terms of how many items are checked off a To Do List each day. If all the items are checked off, they give themselves high marks for time management. If too few items were completed, they may rationalize that the list was too long. Or they may say, "Today wasn't a typical day." Now, before you decide that this is a complaint about To Do Lists, please remember that To Do Lists are indispensable, and they will be examined in great detail later. But To Do Lists are not responsive to unscheduled or unanticipated activities. They also provide little insight about the extent to which other people's priorities control your time. The Time-Use Log overcomes both these problems.

The Time-Use Log provides a telling picture of your time-use patterns—*if* you record your activities honestly. For best results, follow these three guidelines:

1. **All items should be recorded in 15-minute blocks.** There is a good reason for keeping tabs of your time in small increments. Time is used wisely or is wasted in small chunks. Consequently, the accuracy of your time-use picture is enhanced by keeping such detailed records.

2. **List your activities as you do them.** Do not wait until the end of the day to fill out your log. Even the best memory is not up to this task.

3. **Avoid the temptation to make yourself look good by recording what you should be doing instead of what you actually are doing.** It may be painful to record that you spent the last half hour gossiping with a co-worker, but such information is vital to your understanding of where time goes.

The Time-Use Log is more than an impersonal inventory of how much time was devoted to various activities. It is a daily chronicle of your work life presented quantitatively. If the chronicle is written realistically and honestly, a time analysis will reveal both the strengths and weaknesses of your current time-use practices.

Time analysis requires work, but the payoff is worthwhile. The dividends from time analysis can be a lifetime of better control of your time. Expect to be surprised when you examine your Time-Use Log. Your case may be similar to that of one of our consulting clients, a woman we will call Sally Galt.

Sally owns a small jewelry store in suburban Philadelphia with a reputation for personalized attention and reliable service after the sale. Sally conscientiously prepared a daily To Do List, but her list could not keep up with her fast-paced days. Before recording her time, Sally "guesstimated" that she spent 4 hours of her 10-hour day waiting on customers.

Her Time-Use Log told a different story. She actually spent only $1\frac{1}{2}$ hours a day with the public. The majority of her workday was devoted to talking on the telephone with suppliers, creditors, and family members who consulted her on personal matters. Her biggest jolt came when she saw in black and white that the longest period of time she worked without interruption was 20 minutes. Usually the interruptions were much more frequent.

After careful examination of the information, Sally Galt correctly concluded that most of the interruptions were time wasters. She was able to take corrective action to channel more of her time and energy toward her two primary goals of increasing sales in the existing store by 15 percent and opening a new jewelry store before the end of the year.

Begin your own time-use analysis by examining each 15-minute block of time recorded for the first day of your log.

1. Determine whether the activity recorded in a particular block of time was devoted to targeted accomplishment (cell 1), fire fighting (cell 2), other people's priorities (cell 3), or time wasters (cell 4).

2. Place the appropriate number in the box at the end of the line for that activity.

3. Repeat this process for each 15-minute block of time.

4. Add the number of blocks of time devoted to each of the activities and record the number in the appropriate cell in the Time Analysis Grid at the bottom left of the page.

5. Calculate the percentage of time devoted to activities in each of the four cells and record those numbers in the Time Analysis Grid located at the bottom right of the page.

6. Repeat this process for the remaining six days recorded in your Time-Use Log.

Figure 1-2 Time-Use Log

Activity

| 7:00 |
| 7:15 |
| 7:30 |
| 7:45 |
| 8:00 |
| 8:15 |
| 8:30 |
| 8:45 |
| 9:00 |
| 9:15 |
| 9:30 |
| 9:45 |
| 10:00 |
| 10:15 |
| 10:30 |
| 10:45 |
| 11:00 |
| 11:15 |
| 11:30 |
| 11:45 |
| 12:45 |
| 1:00 |
| 1:15 |
| 1:30 |
| 1:45 |
| 2:00 |
| 2:15 |

2:30																		
2:45																		
3:00																		
3:15																		
3:30																		
3:45																		
4:00																		
4:15																		
4:45																		
5:00																		
5:15																		
5:30																		
5:45																		
6:00																		
6:15																		
6:30																		
6:45																		
7:00																		

1 _____	2 _____
Targeted	Fire
Accomplishment	Fighting
3 _____	4 _____
Other People's	Time
Priorities	Wasters

Record *number* of blocks of
time devoted to each activity.

1 _____ %	2 _____ %
Targeted	Fire
Accomplishment	Fighting
3 _____ %	4 _____ %
Other People's	Time
Priorities	Wasters

Calculate *percentage* of time
devoted to each activity.

9

When you completed your analysis you will have a clear picture of your particular time-use pattern. Look at the percentage of time spent on targeted accomplishment. Does it make up less than 50 percent of your day? If so, your investment in this book should pay handsome dividends.

How much of your time was spent fighting fires (cell 2)? If this was more than 15 percent of your time, your planning and organizing skills need to be enhanced. If the fire fighting is caused primarily by your boss, you will need to pay particular attention to the sections devoted to managing your boss.

Examine the time spent on other people's priorities. Did you realize that someone else was in control of such a large percentage of your time? If the percentage of time spent on other people's priorities is greater than 15 percent, you should pay particular attention to the sections of the book that show you how to negotiate relationships with co-workers. It is possible to have cordial relationships with co-workers without losing control of your own priorities.

How much time is devoted to the time wasters of cell 4? Are you satisfied or shocked by the results? If you are shocked, take heart. The time wasters are the quickest and easiest problems to cure with the High-Impact Time Management System.

Finally, take a look at how much time is devoted to unanticipated and/or unimportant activities (cells 2, 3, and 4). If you are like most people, it will be an alarmingly large percentage of the time. If so, it means that your good intentions regarding time management have become overwhelmed by unplanned or urgent, but unimportant, activities.

You have taken the first and most important step in gaining control of your time. You now have a clear picture of your time-use pattern. Consequently, you will be able to pay particular attention to the sections of this book that deal directly with your specific time management problems. The conscientious application of the High-Impact Time Management System will pay dividends every day of your working life.

CHAPTER 2

Become a "Macro" Time Manager

RESISTANCE TO TIME MANAGEMENT

A good friend of mine, Todd Welsch, actively resists all attempts to get him to manage his time more effectively. He insists that he is far more productive than people who "devote their lives to To Do Lists." He has turned his contempt for time management into a set of stories that would make a pretty good night club comedy routine.

Whenever anyone suggests that he could do a better job with controlling his time, he tells elaborate, detailed, and funny stories about the fussy, dull people who are good time managers. These anecdotes always feature "skinny little guys with thick glasses and squeaky voices." Todd's time managers are ardent paper clip counters who make long lists of trivial things to do. Before the story is finished, Todd has painted a picture of a dull, narrow-minded, rigid, unspontaneous person.

The punch line is always the same. When Todd is ready to wind up one of these stories, he shakes his head and says, "This guy's idea of fun is spending Saturday morning organizing the trunk of his car."

Todd's view of time management is a common one. People resist time management because they are afraid they will lose more than they will gain. They fear losing their autonomy and spontaneity. They also feel that they will lose the flexibility and responsiveness necessary to meet unexpected situations. People resist time management because they fear it will reduce their freedom and their effectiveness. In short, they anticipate too much pain for too little gain.

Todd's stereotype suggests that time management turns people into machines. Few people relish the idea of turning their work into assembly-line, piece-rate work. While people can obviously do such work, few prefer it. Much of the resistance to better time management is motivated by a fear of being inflexibly tied to a tightly scheduled list of nitpicking details. For some, such a schedule is about as appealing as staying after school to write "I'll turn my homework in on time" 500 times on the blackboard.

Another popular view depicts time managers as people who cram productive activity into every minute. Life is planned to the minute, and there is little room for leisure or fun. From this perspective, our stereotypical effective time manager could be expected to watch television, read a book, and carry on a conversation at the same time. Similarly, such a person would be expected to dictate correspondence while commuting to work or to read mail while attending a meeting. Countless examples could be cited which suggest that time management takes the life out of work.

If effective time managers really behaved this way, few people indeed would even try to manage their time. The prospect of going to work would be too bleak. Fortunately, effective time managers do not fit the stereotypes just presented. The effective time manager is not a workaholic who sacrifices everything to his or her career. The high-impact time manager is effective at work, devotes time to leisure, and pursues meaningful personal relationships.

MYTHS ABOUT EFFECTIVE TIME MANAGEMENT

The stereotypes of the effective time manager come from a set of myths. Getting serious about time management is difficult until the myths are addressed. To become an effective time manager, you must move beyond the three major time management myths.

Myth 1: Time management is overly concerned with details.

Many people who hate to be bothered with details do almost anything to avoid To Do Lists and other common time management tools. A relatively small proportion of the population responds positively to handling details. A fairly large percentage of people abhor details. While macro management ensures that details are handled appropriately, concern for details is not the major emphasis of the program.

There is no consensus about the importance of attending

to details. On the one hand, we are told "The genius is in the details." On the other hand, we are told "Don't sweat the small stuff." Actually, both are true. Some details are essential and some are trivial. Remembering to check the oil in your car or to put the landing gear down is essential. Responding to a questionnaire from a marketing research firm is probably trivial.

Effective time management concerns distinguishing between essential and trivial details. A good time management system allows you to recognize and respond promptly to the important details. The response can become routine and automatic, which is much less bothersome than is having to deal with it later when it has caused a crisis.

Myth 2: Time management is mechanical.

Time management has a reputation for being mechanical because people focus on a small but visible part of the process. It is easy to see the schedules, lists of deadlines, and timetables of a well-organized person. These portions of any time management system may be mechanical. However, these are the tip of the iceberg and do not reflect what goes into developing the lists and schedules.

Deciding on priorities, enlisting the cooperation and support of other people, and making allowance for unanticipated problems are not mechanical activities. They require considerable insight and creativity. Before attending to details and devising To Do Lists, the high-impact time manager must see the big picture clearly. The type of research and thought that go into understanding the big picture is not mechanical.

Myth 3: Time management reduces flexibility and spontaneity.

Effective time managers devise plans and work hard to see that the plans stay on schedule. This approach produces significant results that cannot be expected when things "take care of themselves." Some people interpret adherence to a plan as inflexibility.

Planning does not necessarily inhibit flexibility. When a plan is not working, a wise person sets it aside and looks for alternative approaches. Unless a plan is overly detailed, many opportunities exist for spontaneous and creative approaches to implementing the plan. The fact that large blocks of time are set aside by effective time managers means that spontaneity and creativity will have an opportunity to flourish.

One of the real advantages of being organized and operating from a plan is that it reduces the degree of urgency faced on a day-to-day basis. Crises and urgency are also enemies of flexibility and spontaneity.

THE MACRO TIME MANAGER

The macro time manager concentrates on the big picture. His or her primary advantage comes from concentrating on tasks worth doing—high-impact tasks. Most people who try to manage their time well get hung up in micro time management. They concentrate on how to do a given task more quickly or more efficiently. They seldom ask whether the task is worth doing in the first place. The macro time manager is relentless in asking that question.

The macro time manager understands that determining what *not* to do is his or her most important task. The macro time manager ruthlessly refuses to become involved in low-impact projects. The best way to save time is to refuse to use it on tasks that have little or no payoff.

The macro time manager has a keen sense of the impact of making choices. A choice to undertake a given project is a decision that inevitably prevents other accomplishments. When the macro time manager says "yes" to one project, he or she realizes that "no" is being said to numerous other possibilities. Thus, choices are made carefully.

The effective macro time manager makes commitments carefully. Commitments are made slowly and deliberately. Because the commitments are made with care, the effective macro time manager is more likely to come through as promised. When becoming involved in projects or selecting daily tasks, the effective macro time manager generally uses a set of standards or rules of thumb for evaluating the importance of tasks. While the standards or rules of thumb applied vary from person to person, most of them focus on the contribution the activity can make to the organization and the individual.

Principle 1: Does this task or project make
a significant contribution to the goals
of the organization?

The number of things that people can get involved in is
infinite. This is true of homemakers and students as well as arc
welders and executives. The number of tasks that have a legitimate claim of our time is almost endless. Never will anyone
ever "get everything done." A recently retired friend remarked
that he was so busy after retirement that he didn't know how
he ever found 40–50 hours a week for his job.

The key is to select tasks or projects that bring great benefit to the organization. These are high-impact tasks or projects.
By picking high-impact projects, the macro time manager in-
vests the world's scarcest resource—time—in a way that will
provide the greatest return on investment.

Principle 2: The Macro Time Manager carefully
evaluates the risks associated with activities.

The payoff for high-impact projects must be judged in
terms of the risks involved. Projects not only have payoffs, they
entail risks. Time, money, effort, and reputations are frequently
on the line when one commits to a project. There is always the
possibility that a new product will be a flop or the new procedure for handling customer complaints will cause more problems than it solves.

People who accomplish things are willing to bear risks.
However, they are not foolhardy or rash. The macro time manager wants to know how bad the worst possible outcome can be.
This is no time for wishful thinking or starry-eyed, positive
thinking. Equally important is an accurate estimate of the
chances that something will go wrong. When the potential problems are well understood, the macro time manager sets out to
neutralize the risks they represent.

While effective time managers may appear optimistic, they
are realists in their estimation of risk. A useful practicality
comes from an accurate understanding of the risks involved in
a given project. The high-impact time manager builds in solutions to problems that are likely to stymie an undertaking. Detailed plans are carefully made. Alternate suppliers may be lined

up just in case. Schedules are arranged with extra care. Progress is monitored regularly, and critical factors are double-checked.

Principle 3: The Macro Time Manager sets priorities.

You will be unable to accomplish all the high-impact tasks that you identify. This is not a fault or a weakness. Simply put, time is a very scarce resource, and many important, worthwhile projects will never be completed or even started. We will not be able to carry through everything we would like to accomplish. Consequently, we must choose, giving one project or task greater priority than other worthy undertakings.

Setting priorities and sticking to them takes self-discipline. We must choose to say "yes" to high-priority goals or tasks even when they are difficult to accomplish. Even more important, we must choose to say "no" to lower-priority goals or tasks. Many of the lower-priority goals are also worthy goals, but they are not important enough to distract us from high-priority tasks.

Our discipline is really challenged when the lower-priority goals appear to be urgent and insistent. When unplanned tasks of great urgency appear on the scene, the macro managers demonstrate their self-discipline. They resist being caught up by the urgency and insistence of the person who brought the project to their attention. The high-impact time manager will be skeptical of anything that disrupts planned, scheduled activities. If it is all that important, why didn't we know about it and plan for it?

The high-impact time manager will have the self-discipline to avoid acting without thinking. He or she will regard this *potential problem* as an unwelcome and probably unnecessary interruption of important and planned work. Before getting involved, the effective macro time manager will make the emerging crisis present its credentials. Is this problem really important? Is this problem really urgent? Is this really *my* problem?

If the problem is not truly important, the macro time manager will simply ignore the problem. If the problem is important but not urgent, response to the problem gets planned and scheduled. If the problem is urgent and important, the high-impact time manager examines the problem to see if it more appropriately belongs to someone else's priority list. If the problem actually belongs to someone else, the high-impact time manager will not take the lead in solving the problem.

> Principle 4: The Macro Time Manager enlists
> the enthusiasm, effort, goodwill, and support
> of other people.

What one person can accomplish is very limited. What a group of people can be coerced to do can be impressive—witness the pyramids. What a team can be inspired to do is unlimited—witness heart transplants and space travel.

The values of independence and going it alone are important to many Americans. However, the values of teamwork and cooperation are of even greater importance. Most tasks are simply too large and interdependent to be accomplished by a single person. Effective managers learn to participate in team efforts and joint ventures. Highly effective managers take the additional step of learning to organize teams and to attract enthusiastic support for their projects.

The most important step for attracting the support of other people is to share your vision with them. People want to be involved in projects that are important. They want to transcend the mundane, everyday duties that constitute most jobs. If you want to enlist people's support, you need to show them how your project fits into the big picture. If they are convinced that your project is exciting and important, you will have supporters. People will enthusiastically add their efforts to yours.

People are also more likely to support you if your project allows them to meet their personal needs. When you ask for cooperation, make it clear what the person can expect in return. At all times, we can offer our gratitude for their efforts. The person who organizes a project should be diligent and generous in giving credit to members of the team for success of the project. Failure to give proper credit will surely dampen enthusiasm when participation in the next project is suggested.

Tom Sawyer gave a bad name to cooperation when he tricked his friends into whitewashing his fence. Mark Twain presented Tom Sawyer as a manipulative, cynical con artist. Motivated by laziness, Tom Sawyer bamboozled his friends into doing his work. Many people fail to involve others because they feel that they may be using Tom Sawyer's trick. However, responsible managers do not trick and manipulate colleagues into doing work that belongs to someone else.

An effective boss will not assign work to a subordinate that legitimately belongs to the boss. When seeking cooperation on a project, the macro time manager expects help only from people who would benefit from the project. Just as the macro time manager resists taking on other people's priorities, he or she expects others to cooperate only when it is consistent with their priorities. Project teams should be composed only of people who see the completion of the project as being mutually beneficial.

The macro time manager is willing to give support as well as ask for it. As long as the requests are consistent with his or her priorities and responsibilities, the macro time manager is a helpful team player. Similarly, the macro time manager is always looking for legitimate allies who can move projects along to completion.

SUMMARY

Many people resist time management techniques. They mistakenly believe that time management will turn them into rigid drones or workaholics. Most of these misconceptions come from a stereotypical portrait of a macro time manager who is concerned with efficiently handling details. Truly effective time managers are macro time managers concerned with the big picture and achieving long-range objectives.

Effective time managers are anything but workaholics. The high-impact time manager accomplishes more in less time. This leaves more time for leisure activities, family, and other personal relationships. The macro time manager takes a balanced approach to his or her career. Effective time management does not tip the balance of activities in favor of more hours at work. Rather, effective time management concentrates on making better use of time in all spheres of life.

CHAPTER 3

Beat the Procrastination Habit

In all too many cases, we are really our own worst enemies when it comes to managing our time. We are frequently well aware of what we should be doing with our time. The high-priority, high-payoff items are clearly identified. The steps that must be taken to accomplish the activity are well known. We have the knowledge and skills required for the job. Yet, somehow, the task never seems to get done. As time goes by, we nag ourselves more and more about what we should be doing. If enough time passes, and we have let numerous opportunities to complete the task slip away, we may even inflict some pretty cruel verbal self-abuse.

Procrastination is the common name given to this problem. The problem, however, is both broader and deeper than the term "procrastination" suggests. The problem is really one of irrational inaction. Most time management books talk about the various forms of procrastination and offer techniques useful for overcoming specific habits of procrastination. Such an approach works as long as we are constantly on the look out for the specific procrastination habits identified by the author. Unfortunately, we procrastinate because we need to procrastinate and are rewarded for doing so. Consequently, new habits of procrastination are formed as quickly as old ones are conquered.

THE CAUSE OF PROCRASTINATION

To solve the problem, we must discover why we procrastinate. In other words, why is it more rewarding to procrastinate than it is to accomplish high-payoff, high-priority tasks?

Procrastination is caused by the situations faced and psychological needs of the person involved. There are several very satisfying rewards for procrastination that are generally unrecognized. While the rewards derived from avoiding difficult or unpleasant tasks are obvious, the rewards derived from waiting until the last minute to begin a pleasant task or a profitable project are less clear. Yet you can be certain that there are rewards.

First, it should be recognized that working frantically to beat a deadline on an important project is exciting. There is a real sense of accomplishment when you hand in that report 5 minutes before the dealine on Friday afternoon. If you had planned ahead, and arranged to hand the report in a day early, the drama, excitement, and sense of accomplishment would not have been as great. In fact, getting the report in a day early makes the whole thing routine and humdrum. Some people are stress junkies who require a fix of adrenaline daily; few things get the adrenaline pumping quicker than facing an important deadline.

Procrastinating on important matters frequently creates crises. And crises reward those who resolve them well. Saving the day can make you a hero. Even though you may have created the crisis in the first place by lack of planning and inaction, coming through in the crunch can sometimes make you look good and feel good. This is a very powerful reward for procrastination.

Boosting one's self-esteem from a personally generated organizational crisis is immature and irresponsible. Thriving on the stress of meeting deadlines is part of the excitement inherent in many fast-paced, demanding jobs. However, generating the stress through procrastination coupled with frantic, last-minute efforts to meet the deadline is not only poor time management but irresponsible behavior.

Now, let's look at some of the kinds of things that we know we should be doing but simply put off repeatedly. Some are tasks that are inherently unpleasant. Such things might include going to the dentist, figuring income taxes, calling a slow-paying customer to collect a bill, conducting a performance appraisal with an employee who is a marginal performer, cleaning the gutters, or completing tedious paperwork. These tasks are in and of themselves punishing. Any reasonably busy person can find countless legitimate tasks that are more pleasant to do. With hardly any effort at all, we can be "too busy" to get around to the necessary but unpleasant parts of the job.

The second type of task that leads to procrastination is the large project that is important but not urgent. Since the project is large, it will require setting aside several sizable blocks of time. Considerable detailed planning will have to go into organizing the people and resources needed to complete the project.

Examples of important but not urgent projects would include updating the personnel procedures manual, conducting customer satisfaction research on customers who had switched to a competitor, landscaping the yard, revising the performance appraisal system, conducting a study that would compare the company's current health insurance program with other available plans, and remodeling the recreation room at home. None of these projects is particularly unpleasant, and there is little uncertainty about how to get the job done. The real problem is the amount of time required for the projects. While these are legitimate—even important—projects, few of us ever set aside sufficient time to complete them without the pressure of a deadline.

The third type of task that causes procrastination is the creative project. Occasionally, we get the opportunity to do something that is a real stretch in terms of our talents, something that requires real creativity, resourcefulness, or originality. The payoff from such a project can be very high. Such projects are opportunities to stand out and showcase our talents. However, they are also chances to fail spectacularly.

The procrastinator also bears personal responsibility for his or her inaction. Certain habits and situations foster procrastination. Habits of overinvolvement, overcommitment, disorganization, and attention to minutiae promote busyness while deflecting attention from high-priority items. Failure to protect ourselves from drop-in visitors, unscreened phone calls, and overly long meetings also promote procrastination.

CONQUERING DISTASTEFUL TASKS

The rewards of procrastination on inherently distasteful tasks are obvious. As long as the task is put off, the unpleasantness is avoided. We also cherish the irrational hope that maybe there will be some way to avoid the task all together. Perhaps the poor-performing employee will quit, maybe tomorrow's mail will bring a check from that slow-paying customer, or there is always the chance that a really hard rain will wash the leaves from the gutter. Unfortunately, hoping and waiting does little for taking care of the necessary but unpleasant tasks.

Inherently distasteful tasks are prime candidates for procrastination. Learning how to attack these tasks can add tremendously to your effectivess. Some of these tasks, such as conducting performance appraisals and visiting the dentist, will respond to scheduling. It is much more difficult to put off a visit to the dentist if you schedule your next appointment while still at the dentist's office for your current checkup. Similarly, performance appraisals can be scheduled annually on the anniversary of the subordinate's first day of employment. Schedule next year's appointment with your tax accountant when you do this year's taxes.

A surprising number of necessarily unpleasant activities are amenable to scheduling. When a task is scheduled, it is much more difficult to avoid. Breaking an appointment takes effort and is also unpleasant, perhaps almost as unpleasant as going through with the nasty task. The simple act of writing a task on your schedule enhances its importance, legitimacy, and urgency. When a scheduled activity is accomplished and checked off the list, you can generally expect a sense of satisfaction, or at least relief.

A good way to deal with small, nagging distasteful tasks is simply to do them. Make it a habit to start each morning by attacking a small, nasty job. An early-morning accomplishment can give you the psychological boost needed to tackle larger, more demanding tasks later in the day. Getting an unpleasant task out of the way early in the day can set the tone for a productive day. If you spend a good portion of your day dreading and avoiding a distasteful task, you will find it impossible to concentrate your efforts on your other high-priority tasks.

When your mind is filled with dread, you are likely to spend your time switching from one low-priority task to another throughout the day. At the end of the day, you may be exhausted, but you will be hard pressed to point out the day's accomplishments. Even those things accomplished are likely to be fairly low-priority items.

W. Clement Stone, billionaire insurance executive and founder of *Success* magazine, banishes procrastination with positive affirmations. "Do it NOW!" he shouts. Employing Stone's approach, you can startle yourself out of your mental ruts. Acting on affirmations, you can overwhelm your tendency to procrastinate with immediate action. Stone recommends including such positive affirmations in your ongoing mental dialogue with yourself. According to Stone, your internal self-talk should always be a pep talk. The momentum of completing the job can snowball into a full day of accomplishment.

Another approach in grappling with the generally distasteful task is to couple it with a pleasant task. In this way you can use the pleasant task as a reward for completing the undesirable one. For example, you may be facing some tedious paperwork and find it almost impossible to get started. However, you could link finishing the paperwork with the far more pleasant task of shopping several department stores to see how your competitor's products are displayed and priced.

Similarly, you might reward yourself with the purchase of a book, item of clothing, or a special lunch when you have completed a particularly onerous job. Small rewards, used to break through the procrastination habit, can pay large dividends in terms of effective time management.

DEALING WITH OVERWHELMINGLY LARGE PROJECTS

The rewards of procrastination for the second type of task, the large, important, but not urgent project, are more subtle and complex. The payoff for large, important projects is usually clear. The biggest problem is that the payoff or reward is distant.

Completing any project, large or small, produces gratification and satisfaction. When the project is a large one, it takes a long time to complete it, and the gratification is delayed. Most people have difficulty delaying gratification when immediate rewards are available. Consequently, a smaller, less important, but more urgent task gets completed. A smaller, but more immediate, gratification is received. In this case, small, immediate rewards drive out large, delayed rewards.

Two approaches are effective in getting action on large projects. First, you can increase the urgency of the project. If the project is really important, you and your associates can establish a deadline for its completion. The deadline will give the project more urgency in your own mind.

A public announcement of your commitment to complete the project by your deadline is another way to increase urgency. Second, you can make the project more immediately rewarding. Break the project down into smaller tasks. Reward yourself when you complete each of the these smaller tasks. Now the path to completing the large, important project is marked by rewarding milestones along the way. The large project with little urgency has been transformed into a series of small, urgent, and immediately rewarding tasks.

WHEN THE CREATIVE PRESSURE IS ON

The rewards for procrastinating on creative projects are more difficult to see. Most people enjoy being considered creative and innovative, but they fear that they are not. If you complete a project that obviously requires creativity or resourcefulness, your creativity is open to evaluation. Any illusions you or others may hold about your creative talents may be subjected to a painful reexamination.

Fear of negative evaluation can cause paralysis at any and every stage of the project. Some are so fearful and unsure of their abilities that they cannot even start a creative project. Others have no trouble getting started, but find it impossible to finish. Even those celebrated for their creativity may suffer from insecurities about their talents. When it comes to creative work, past triumphs do not guarantee future successes.

Overcoming procrastination on creative projects is particularly difficult because the inaction is motivated by deep-seated and largely irrational fears and insecurities. While we cannot begin to offer solutions for the fears and insecurities that block creative work, we can provide some straightforward advice for moving creative projects ahead in spite of fears and insecurities. The following three approaches produce excellent results:

1. Make the creative task less intimidating and psychologically threatening.
2. Establish routine work procedures and follow them

even when the creative juices are not flowing. Getting started is half done.

3. Share the creative burden by involving others in your project. Make the creative project a collaborative effort by asking others for their insights, advice, and help.

Do not be unduly intimidated when creativity and resourcefulness are required to complete a project. It is easy to make too big of a deal of the importance of creativity. Even a project which hinges on a brilliant insight requires far more perspiration than inspiration. If you do not feel immediately creative, start with the necessary low-level work. Immersion in the details of the project is often enough to spark a creative insight that will reveal a useful, innovative approach to the problem.

Inhibiting fears can be reduced by putting the task at hand in perspective. Most of the projects we procrastinate about do not demand the creativity necessary to work on frontiers of art, science, and literature. You have not been asked to paint the Sistine Chapel, develop a cure for cancer, or write a sonnet. If your task is to produce a new advertising campaign for a deodorant soap, remind yourself that you are not writing the great American novel. It is also useful to note that perfection on the first try is not required. Whatever you do can be revised, reworked, and modified as needed.

The second approach to overcoming procrastination on creative projects is to develop a routine for doing creative work. Very little creative work would be accomplished if people worked only when they felt creative. Waiting for the urge to strike or the mood to be right will virtually guarantee failure. Ironically, even the most creative people regularly have rigid and demanding work schedules. They work when they feel inspired and when they do not. For example, science fiction writer Frederick Pohl prevents writer's block by setting a three-page-a-day writing quota for himself. Pohl forces himself to meet his quota 365 days a year.

The third approach, involving others in your creative projects, makes particular sense when you are already part of a team within an organization. Most large projects completed in an organization require the efforts of numerous people in any case. Why not let others share in the burdens and rewards of creativity?

Many of the tactics which can effectively stimulate creativity naturally benefit from collaborative effort. Research on problem solving suggests that groups frequently do a better job of solving problems than individuals working alone. This is particularly true when the problems are unusual and lie outside the expertise of anyone in the group. Brainstorming, for example, is far more productive when several people of diverse backgrounds are involved.

Procrastination takes many forms, but quite often it is motivated by some form of insecurity. We put off tasks that we are afraid will produce unpleasant outcomes or are unpleasant in themselves. When we fear unpleasant outcomes, it is usually because we are insecure about our abilities to produce the desired result. We may lack the skills needed for the job at hand. Or we may fear that we lack the insight and creativity to solve a particularly thorny or perplexing problem. In most cases, there are fairly straightforward ways for dealing with these problems.

Decisiveness seems to be the opposite of procrastination. The problem here seems to be one of **when** to act. When one acts at the appropriate time, a reputation for decisiveness is earned. When one acts prematurely, one is labeled rash. When a person is slow to act, he or she is frequently considered a procrastinator. The key element is timing. As in so many of life's endeavors, timing is essential. Success in most athletic events depends on timing measured in milliseconds. Ice skaters leaping into a triple jump must have their movements timed to the split second. A quarterback throwing a 40-yard pass to a receiver must have an equally well-developed sense of timing.

Timing is also important for those performing sales, supervisory, or managerial tasks. The effective salesperson must learn the right moment to close the sale. The supervisor needs to know when to provide instruction to the new employee and when to let the employee struggle with a new task. And the manager must know how to sequence a variety of tasks to bring a large project to conclusion on time.

The timing required in most work is not as critical or precise as the examples just provided. However, timing does play a critical role in a variety of jobs. When delegating a task, you and your subordinate need to have a realistic view of how long the assignment is going to take. Otherwise, costly delays are likely. When ordering inventory, one must be aware of how quickly the various items in inventory are selling and how long it will take for items to be delivered after they are ordered.

GAMES PROCRASTINATORS PLAY

Most of us are pretty good at playing games in which we end up fooling ourselves. There are several procrastination games that guarantee frustration and failure. The most popular procrastination game is a "when" game. "I'll get to that *when* . . .".

The *when* sentence can be completed in a variety of ways. I'll get to that when

I'm not so busy.
I have more time.
I have more information.
our kids are grown.
I'm out of debt.
things aren't so hectic.
the time is right.
I'm good and ready.

All these responses mean the same thing: "I'm going to ignore a legitimate, important task until it goes away or I'm forced to do it." Most of them are merely polite ways to say "Go away, can't you see I'm busy?"

"When" games can be difficult to deal with because they are excuses for procrastination that sound valid, even prudent. In fact the reward derived from playing "when" games is guilt reduction. When you have a good reason for postponing action, it is not necessary to feel guilty about your inaction. Better yet, the excuses sound so plausible not even your boss or your spouse can fault you for postponing a particular task to a more appropriate time. Unfortunately, the "appropriate time" never comes for most of the activities delayed by "when" games. Look closely to see if you can recognize yourself in some of the "when" games described next.

The most frequent "when" game is called "When I Have More Time." Almost all of us are skilled players at this game. The truth is that we never have more time. You see, time is nicely partitioned into 60-second minutes, 60-minute hours, 24-hour days, 7-day weeks, 52-week years, and 10-year decades. Getting "more" simply doesn't exist.

An interesting variation of the "When I Have More Time" game is called the Grand Daydream, and it works something like this. Jay Skidmore is a bright young operations analyst with a new degree in economics. He is eager to demonstrate that he is not only competent but brilliant. Jay has just received an assignment from Barbara Moody, his boss. She asked Skidmore to review the company's health plan to see if the premiums are in line with the benefits provided by the plan. So far, so good.

Skidmore takes on the job eagerly, seeing it as an opportunity to make a big hit with the boss. Not only will he check out the current plan against similar coverage from other insurers, but he plans to collect information on plans with better coverage *and* better prices. When he has all this information in hand, Skidmore plans to present his findings in a bound report filled with presentation-quality graphics.

This is a fine idea, except for one small detail. Skidmore has turned a four-hour project into a three-day project. If he had the free time, that might be fine. But his other commitments are significant and pressing. Since he wants to surprise his boss with an unexpectedly impressive report, he does not share his redefinition of the project with her. Consequently, he is expected to continue with all his current duties.

Since Skidmore now thinks of the project as large and time consuming, he cannot find a simple, straightforward way to tackle the project. After a couple of false starts, our would-be hero decides that he doesn't have time to complete the entire project this week. But next week comes, and there are still no sufficiently large blocks of free time to complete the project.

Meanwhile, more urgent demands have captured his attention, and the study of the health insurance plan gets put on a back burner. At the same time, the boss has concluded that Skidmore can't be counted on to handle even a small project in a timely fashion. Jay's grandiose daydreams robbed him of a solid, if mundane, accomplishment that could have been well regarded by his boss. Skidmore has become the victim of the Grand Daydream.

A similar game is called "I Can Do a Better Job Later." In this case, the procrastinator does not change the nature or scope of the task. The issue is the quality of the job done. Our procrastinator wants to do a good job but is doubtful about the delivery of the quality needed. Instead of dealing with this problem head on, the procrastinator puts off the task until "I have the time to do it right." But there is probably not going to be any more time later than there is now. In fact, there may be less time, particularly if the task involves a deadline. Few tasks can be accomplished more easily or with higher quality simply because the procrastinator waits longer to get started.

A third procrastination game is called "We Need More Information." This is a particularly difficult game to recognize because it is often true that more information is required to make an appropriate decision. Mike Adams edits a lively, informative newsletter for the customers of a growing engineering design firm. The crisp, professional-looking layout is accentuated by the high-quality paper used to print the newsletter. The only trouble is that the newsletter is too expensive.

In an effort to cut costs, Adams begins to look for different graphic artists, printers, mailing services, and sources of paper. He manages to get quotes from one or more vendors on each item. Not all the vendors can supply exactly the same services provided by the current vendor who provides a turn-key job. Consequently, it is not possible to compare "apples to apples" in all respects.

Rather than make the decision about whether or not to switch production to new graphic artists, typesetters, and printers, Adams procrastinates, telling himself and his boss that he "needs more information" before he can make a decision. However, he is not spending any time or effort collecting bids from different vendors. He is merely procrastinating.

TACTICS FOR BEATING THE PROCRASTINATION HABIT

Norman Vincent Peale, renowned minister, prolific writer, and public speaker, confesses to procrastination problems early in his career. Unwilling to hurt people's feelings, Peale tended to overcommit himself. Having committed himself to projects that held little appeal, Peale tended to procrastinate and then work at a frenzied pace. As a consequence, he worked himself to the point of exhaustion while still failing to fulfill all his commitments.

As a result of his own problems, Dr. Peale developed a five-point strategy for breaking the procrastination habit:

1.   Pick one problem area for procrastination and work on it exclusively until it is under control. The cold turkey approach to beating the procrastination habit is doomed to failure. If your immediate goal is to eliminate procrastination in areas of your life, you will find it overwhelming and unattainable. However, the goal of promptly starting on your weekly sales report and completing it on time is a manageable, attainable goal.

After you have conquered your tendency to procrastinate about the weekly sales report, you are ready to attack your tendency to put off your other paperwork responsibilities. After one area is under control, you are ready to move to another.

2.   Set priorities and focus on one problem at a time. Remember that you will never have enough time to respond to all the legitimate claims on your time. Since you can't possibly satisfy all the demands on your time, it is crucial to devote your efforts to high-priority tasks. Without priorities, you jump from task to task, ignoring major responsibilities while wasting time on trivial matters.

Establishing priorities focuses your attention on fewer, but more important, things. Dealing with problems one at a time focuses your attention and energy. You get more done in less time, and fewer things are put aside and simply forgotten.

3.   Set deadlines for yourself. A deadline, like a priority, focuses attention and energy on a particular task. Many people who seem to thrive on stress can generate enormous amounts of enthusiastic effort as a major deadline approaches. In many areas you can beat procrastination simply by setting a deadline and sticking to it.

4.   Do not try to avoid the most difficult problems. Attack the toughest problem first. Dealing effectively with a difficult problem banishes fear and dread while building the confidence required to meet the other challenges of the day.

5.   Do not let perfectionism paralyze you. You will frequently face situations in which 90 percent of the possible benefit from a task is gained from the first 20 percent of the effort expended. A perfectionist will spend an additional 70 percent of his or her time to improve the results from 90 percent to 95 percent. Economists refer to this phenomenon as the law of diminishing returns. A good time manager can judge whether or not the investment of additional time in a project is going to provide a sufficient return.

The perfectionist is never satisfied by results that could be termed "sufficient," "average," or "good enough." The danger of perfectionism lies in the amount of time and effort required to make the assignment "perfect." As a consequence, he or she misses opportunities, becomes overworked, and grows disenchanted with a free market system that seems to value quantity over quality.

SUMMARY

Procrastination takes many forms and is often difficult to identify as the cause of time management problems. People procrastinate because they find certain rewards in putting off work they know they should be doing. Some of the rewards of procrastinating include the excitement of meeting a deadline at the very last second, postponing or avoiding disagreeable tasks, and delaying negative judgments about performance on challenging tasks.

A variety of techniques are available to overcome procrastination. Many tasks that we have a tendency to put off can be readily accomplished if they are simply scheduled. When a task is scheduled, we have a tendency to complete it. We can quit procrastinating on large projects by breaking them down into smaller tasks that are more manageable. Creative projects can be managed by establishing routine work procedures and involving others in our efforts.

CHAPTER 4

Eliminating
Time
Wasters

Wasting time exacts a huge economic toll. Interoffice memos, constantly ringing telephones, drop-in visitors and the inability to delegate authority are typical time-wasters that reduce productivity and lead to one crisis after another.

Spread over the entire national economy, interruptions and other time wasters are a multibillion-dollar-a-year problem that, until recently, went virtually ignored. The strength of the Japanese economy and the growing power of other Pacific rim countries is forcing American corporations to look for every way possible to increase productivity.

As consultants, we have worked with thousands of people who report being victimized by common time-wasting activities. The most common time wasters are

1. Telephone interruptions
2. Drop-in visitors
3. Meetings
4. Procrastination
5. Paperwork
6. Indecision

How many of these time wasters apply to you? If you're like most people, you probably experience them all from time to time. But that doesn't mean they're inevitable. You can control them by knowing exactly when the interruptions occur and under what conditions.

The problem of time wasters fits into cell 4 of the Time Analysis Grid. The time devoted to these tasks is almost a complete loss in terms of effective accomplishment. To determine whether or not a task is a time waster, apply two tests. If the activity is (1) unanticipated and (2) unimportant, it is a time waster. For some people, up to 60 percent of the day can be consumed by time wasters. Ruthless tactics are justified to eliminate time wasters from your day.

One of the major time wasters is the telephone. While it is

an extremely useful tool, the telephone can be a constant interruption. Here are some ways to deal with it:

1. Have someone qualify your incoming calls. Have a
    family member or your secretary offer to help the caller
    on routine matters. Don't be afraid simply to let the
    telephone ring. Answering a phone under any and all
    conditions may be proper etiquette, but in some cases
    it's highly unproductive.

2. A marketing consultant who is a friend of ours has
    more pressing appointments than anyone I've ever
    seen. Whenever a long-winded caller drones on he cuts
    him off by saying that he has a crucial appointment or
    deadline coming up.

3. Social small talk is a great icebreaker, but it doesn't
    have to drag on endlessly. You'll waste less time if you
    cut through the chitchat as soon as possible. Get to the
    point and stick to it.

4. Group your calls so you can choose the time of day
    when people are most likely to be in. Making repeat
    calls to the same number at various times throughout
    the day causes unnecessary interruptions that reduce
    productivity.

5. Analyze every telephone call to see who *ends* the con-
    versation. If it is all too frequently the person on the
    other end of the phone, then you are not in control. Gain
    control—now.

6. Don't be reluctant to get the help of others in your ef-
    forts to make productive use of the telephone. Tell peo-
    ple who call you regularly when you prefer to receive
    calls. Ask those you telephone when they prefer to be
    called.

7. Use telephone answering machines, when appropriate.
    While some people hate talking at the tone, answering
    machines do permit you to receive and return calls on
    your terms.

DEALING WITH DROP-IN VISITORS

They drop in from the blue, unannounced and sometimes thoroughly unwelcome. Drop-in visitors appear at your door at the

worst possible time: at 9:00 P.M. April 15 while you're trying to unravel the mysteries of the federal income tax system by the midnight deadline, at 2:45 P.M. as you are trying to get ready for a 3:00 meeting, and we could go on and on.

Drop-ins are almost unavoidable, but they needn't beat a path to your door if you know how to handle them with honesty and openness. If someone asks you "Got a minute?" say "No." Saying "No" shows you're serious about time management.

1. Who says that all meetings must be held in your home or office? Go to the other party's office if he or she absolutely must see you—you'll have control of when to leave.

2. Arrange your office furniture so you are not facing the flow of traffic. People are most apt to drop in if they can catch your eye.

3. Close your door for some quiet time. You can do anything you want—work, read, relax, or meditate—just as long as you have some time for yourself and the work at hand.

4. Encourage the use of appointments. The people meeting with you will have more respect for your time if an appointment is needed. You will also have more opportunity to be well-prepared to meet the needs of those who need to see you.

THE MEETING MORASS

Organizations mean meetings. It doesn't matter if it's a meeting of the board of directors of a major company or a gathering of the neighborhood garden club; chances are you have vivid memories of a supposed 30-minute session that somehow turned into a 3-hour ordeal.

It is true that most meetings are horribly run. They lack direction and purpose. They ramble on, sometimes degenerating into gripe sessions that don't produce tangible results.

Despite our best intentions, meetings are huge time wasters. But since they're inevitable, it's to our advantage to run or participate in them as efficiently and profitably as possible.

If you're serious, or even mildly interested in getting the most from your meetings, the hints listed here are for you:

1. Show some guts by sticking to a schedule. Obtain everyone's commitment to arrive on time; then start promptly. Don't wait for everyone to arrive, even senior management.

2. Have a specific purpose for calling or attending the meeting. With very few exceptions, meetings should not be called for a general purpose, such as to discuss marketing programs or to discuss family finances.

3. Compile and distribute to participants an agenda with specific topics. Read necessary materials and collected data before, not during, the meeting.

4. Place a time frame for all meetings or conferences. Hold your meetings in a room with a clearly visible clock. Timepieces have a great way of encouraging brevity.

5. Have someone at the meeting take notes so a summary of the discussions can be typed and distributed to participants. If the meeting isn't important enough to justify a summary, it shouldn't have been called.

6. Meetings can be improved if a few minutes are spent critiquing each one after it's over. Discuss the agenda, whether participants came prepared for discussion, the clarity of their comments, and so on.

SURVIVING THE PAPERWORK EPIDEMIC

Everyone complains about paperwork, but despite the griping we sometimes overlook one important fact: not all paperwork is of equal importance. Once created, however, reports, summaries, analyses, and other standard business forms seem to take on a life of their own. They become a product of tradition and habit, and they seem to be equally demanding of our time and attention regardless of their true importance.

The key to dealing with paperwork is to separate the important material from the trivial. Important paperwork has a direct bearing on your personal success and achievement or the effectiveness of the organization. It monitors, controls, informs, educates, or motivates.

Nonessential paperwork contains "nice to know" information that may be helpful if you're playing "Trivial Pursuit," but your life won't be adversely affected if you don't read it.

You can reduce the paperwork in your office by

1. Using a dictating machine. Dictate your key thoughts into one, and let your secretary compose the letters.
2. Before writing anything, ask yourself, "Does this need to be put in writing?"
3. Make sure your correspondence is adequate, not perfect. This doesn't mean sending memos full of typographical errors. It does mean not going overboard on detail.
4. Keep written messages short. Eliminate unnecessary words, sentences, and so on. There's nothing wrong with one-paragraph memos.
5. Plan what you're going to write or dictate. Make an outline of key points you want to address.
6. Answer letters by making handwritten responses at the bottom or in the margin of the letter and mailing it back to the sender.
7. Keep your desk clean. "I have it here somewhere" is the cry of a disorganized person bogged down by paperwork.
8. After initial sorting, handle paper only once. Do it yourself, delegate it, or discard it.

CONCLUSION

The primary thing to remember about time wasters is that they steal time in little chunks. When you get to the end of the day and have trouble remembering where the time went, your day has been filled with time wasters. You need to keep constantly alert for time wasters and act promptly and decisively to eliminate them from your day. Single-minded vigilance exercised against time wasters is needed to preserve your time for higher and better uses.

CHAPTER 5

Saying "No" to Other People's Priorities

The hectic, fragmented workday experienced by most of us makes it difficult to stick to our priorities. During any given day, we may have to interact with dozens of people. Many of them will make unexpected requests that could consume considerable time. Saying "yes" to all these requests would be disastrous. Our own priorities would be completely displaced by the priorities of other people.

Some of the time requested by other people legitimately belongs to them, and we need to respond. Other requests are unfair and inappropriate. The difficulty is distinguishing between the two. This chapter provides you with guidelines for deciding when to play on someone else's team and when to stick to your own priorities.

PRIORITIES: YOURS AND OTHER PEOPLE'S

Your daily activities need to be governed by your long-term objectives. As noted in the chapter on "macro time management," the high-impact time manager integrates long-term goals, intermediate goals, and daily tasks. The integration procedure guarantees that every day's activities make at least some contribution to long-term goals.

The items on your To Do List that contribute to your long-term goals are "priority" items. Anything that distracts you from these priority items threatens your long-term goals. Vigilance is required to protect the time you need to devote to the priority items on your To Do List.

Your co-workers also have priorities. They have pressing projects that need to be completed. The completion of some of these projects may absolutely require your cooperation and participation. Other projects may not *require* your participation, but their completion would be greatly accelerated by your cooperative efforts. Still other requests for your help may seem far removed from your responsibilities and priorities.

As is the case with most people in these situations, you

probably find yourself providing more assistance to others than you would prefer. You may feel tricked, trapped, or manipulated into spending your time in ways that benefit others far more than it benefits you. Your priorities have been displaced by someone else's. You have enhanced someone else's effectiveness to the detriment of your own.

You may recognize the problem but not know how to solve it. While you resent having your own priorities displaced, you may find it difficult to refuse a direct request for assistance. Saying "No" makes you feel guilty.

You may have trouble recognizing manipulative tactics and responding to them appropriately. If you are regularly the victim of other people's priorities, it may be because you have trouble asserting yourself. If you feel manipulated frequently, you may be attempting to protect your self-esteem from those who use guilt, putdowns, and criticism to get their own way at your expense.

PROTECTING YOUR SELF-ESTEEM

Your self-esteem should be secure as you interact with people. At no point should you allow your self-esteem to be diminished by anyone. No one has the right to judge your worth as a human being. You can perform effectively only to the extent that you feel that you are a worthwhile person. Any interaction that calls that worth into question devalues you and causes you to operate defensively.

You need to learn to work with other people without compromising your self-esteem. You will find that some of your coworkers may attempt to take unfair advantage of you in terms of getting you to commit to fulfilling their priorities. This concept is more clearly understood if we look at the different ways cooperation can be elicited.

Cooperation can be gained by striking a mutually beneficial deal. This type of relationship depends on reciprocity and a mutual respect for the rights and needs of all parties. This type of relationship is essentially healthy and promotes effectiveness as well as psychological health.

Contrast this approach with attempts to motivate action

through threats and intimidation. Almost everyone recognizes that threats of bodily harm are unacceptable ways to motivate people either at work or at home. Most people simply will not put up with intimidation. There are too many other places to work and too many other people who can be your friends.

Between these two approaches you find the manipulator. The manipulator would never threaten bodily harm and never attempt to intimidate you physically. The manipulator's tactics are more subtle and insidious. It is not your body that is attacked, it is your mind. Specifically, the manipulator threatens your self-esteem in an effort to gain compliance you would not likely grant freely. Unless your self-esteem is extremely strong and well defended, the tactics of the manipulator are very effective.

The manipulator specializes in making you feel anxious, insecure, fearful, and guilty. The manipulator threatens to pass judgment, finding you inadequate and unworthy. If you comply with the manipulator's demands, judgment is delayed, and temporarily you are allowed to continue to feel worthy. You get to feel OK about yourself until the next time the manipulator needs something.

In plain language this is an extortion racket. Your self-esteem should not be held hostage to anyone else's opinion. Certainly you should not have to give into other people's demands for your help or your time to keep your self-esteem intact.

To maintain control of your time and stick to your priorities, you must be able to recognize and defend against manipulative tactics. Your first line of defense is to recognize what is happening to you. The manipulator has a tendency to

- Put people down.
- Criticize others' performance.
- Point out mistakes.
- Use the word "should" often.
- Threaten to withdraw approval.

Anyone who couples a request for assistance with an implied threat is attempting to manipulate you. Anyone who attacks your self-esteem should receive no cooperation from you.

Cooperating when your self-esteem is under attack merely reinforces behavior that is destructive to you. Your refusal to cooperate on that basis sends the message that you will not be manipulated.

Most people are afraid to refuse to cooperate with a manipulator. They fear the manipulator's disapproval. A person with fragile self-esteem is afraid to lose anyone's goodwill—even the goodwill of a person who is trying to harm them. However, refusal to respond to manipulation is essential.

When you refuse to be manipulated, you send an important message: This won't work with me. The manipulator now has two choices: (1) Do without your assistance or (2) learn to deal with you in a mutually beneficial way. In either case, you are a winner because you have been able to protect your self-esteem.

Here are some tactics that will allow you to defend your self-esteem while refusing to be distracted by other people's priorities.

Tactic 1: Acknowledge the other person's feelings but say "No" firmly.

An inappropriate request for assistance should be turned down in a friendly but firm fashion. You could say, "I see your problem, but I won't be able to help." Or you might say, "I understand how you feel, but I'm not available to help."

People do not automatically have a claim on your time. Their need does not create an obligation on you. If the request is in your best interests, you may decide to cooperate. If the request is in the best interest of the organization, you may decide to cooperate. However, you are not obligated to cooperate in any case.

Tactic 2: Subject every request for your time to the priority test.

Screen every request for your time with the following questions.

- Is this request compatible with my long-term priorities?

- Is this request compatible with the long-term priorities of my department or division?
- Is this request compatible with the long-term priorities of the organization?

If the answer to all three questions is "No," you should absolutely refuse the request. Refuse it politely but firmly. If the answer to the first question is "No" and the answer to the other two questions is "Yes," you should refuse the request unless the benefits to the organization or your department are overwhelming.

Tactic 3: When asked to work on a project outside your area, ask who has primary responsibility for the task.

When a project resides in another department, do not provide assistance that transfers the responsibility to you. If you take on a job that really belongs to someone else, you have let them off the hook and put yourself on the hook. This is almost never a wise move.

Tactic 4: Refuse to feel guilty.

Guilt is the manipulator's most common weapon. The manipulator will attempt to make you feel guilty in areas where you have no control or responsibility. Consider the classic we all heard as kids: "Clean your plate because there are hungry kids in Africa who would love to have that food."

Let's look at that "logic" for a minute. The kid can't throw away food because someone 5,000 miles away is hungry? Will eating the food left on the plate make hungry kids in Africa any less hungry? Will throwing the food away make the African kids more hungry? Of course not. This discourse is not about hungry kids. It is about power and control. The parent has used guilt to control the child. The hidden message here is, "You should do what I say or I will decide you are not a nice person." This is the basic logic of guilt.

SUMMARY

Our priorities provide guidelines for allocating time on a daily basis. Although we are busy with our own priorities, numerous other people make daily attempts to enlist our aid in accomplishing their priorities. Unless we are careful, our own priorities will be displaced by theirs.

When people ask for our assistance based on reciprocity, mutual respect, and mutual benefit, healthy and productive relationships can develop. But compliance obtained through manipulation is a destructive racket. We can use assertive behavior to short-circuit manipulation and counteract the tendency to get bogged down in other people's problems and priorities.

CHAPTER 6

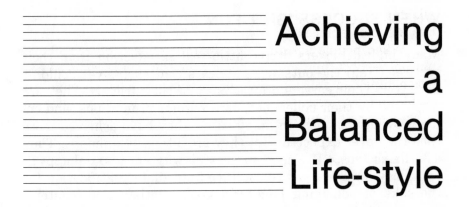

Achieving
a
Balanced
Life-style

WHEN SUCCESS ISN'T FUN

Many high achievers derive little real satisfaction from their success. From the outside, it appears that their lives couldn't be better. Their careers are the envy of their friends. They are respected by their colleagues, earn regular promotions, and enjoy growing incomes. In many cases, they have achieved more than they ever expected. But they are intensely unhappy. They ask themselves, "If I'm so successful, why am I so unhappy?"

They have learned to sacrifice immediate gratification for the sake of achieving long-term goals. Satisfaction, contentment, and happiness were expected as rewards for success. Current sacrifices were expected to produce greater satisfactions "later." But it *is* later. And the ease and enjoyment expected from having "made it" are not there. To make matters worse, they feel somewhat guilty about how well they have done, and even more guilty for being unhappy.

High achievers who are intensely unhappy are probably suffering from career burnout. A person suffering from career burnout feels he or she is making enormous investments in his or her career and is not getting enough back from the efforts expended. The phenomenon was first recognized as occurring among professionals in the helping occupations such as nursing, teaching, and counseling.

Those in the helping professions make large emotional investments in their jobs and their clients. Quite frequently, they get very little in return emotionally for their efforts. They report feeling that they give and give and give but get little in return. The results of this imbalance is an emotional exhaustion called burnout.

Burnout affects people in all occupations. While burnout is more likely in some occupations, no occupation is immune. The real cause of burnout is not the situation, but our response to the situation. We can take steps both on and off the job to prevent burnout. The people who respond positively to the demands and stresses of their life achieve a balanced life-style.

Achievers leading a fast-paced life sometimes have a difficult time deciding whether they are burned out or just busy. People suffering from burnout tend to experience some or all of the following symptoms:

- They feel tired almost all the time—even after a full night's sleep.
- They find that leisure is not relaxing.
- They "have everything" but feel like a failure.
- They do not feel as emotionally close to people as they once did.
- They work frantically but feel as if they are moving in slow motion.
- They feel out of control and unable to cope with even small stressful events at work or home.
- They want to be left alone.

If you have experienced several of these symptoms, there is a good chance that you have some degree of career burnout. Fortunately, the High-Impact Time Management System can help you deal with burnout. A great deal of emphasis has been placed on setting priorities and achieving your goals. Most of our examples have been work examples. As a consequence, it may appear that we believe that all work and no play makes Jack successful. Yet, nothing could be further from the truth.

We do not take the position that work is inherently good. Nor do we take the position that play and leisure are a waste of time. While work provides some intrinsic satisfactions, a life filled with work alone is likely to be unhappy and, ultimately, unproductive. The workaholic is not our model of the effective time manager. In fact, the workaholic may use time very ineffectively. Since workaholics know that they will be putting in many more hours than the average person, they may feel little need to make each hour count.

Leisure is not idleness. Leisure is the pursuit of activities or pastimes that are inherently interesting. Leisure is activity that is tied to our deepest values and interests. Play is an essentially human way of encountering the world. Play is experimental, casual, and easygoing. Children learn some of the most complex things in life through play. They learn to walk, talk, ride vehicles, assume different roles, and achieve fairness through play. While leisure and play may require great expenditures of energy, they are seldom tiring or stressful. Play and leisure provide renewal.

Long hours do not necessarily spell accomplishment. What is put into each hour counts a great deal. With physical work, effectiveness diminishes significantly when a person works more than 8 hours a day. With intellectual work, the fall-off in effectiveness caused by long hours is not as clear, but it is definitely there. At the end of a 14-hour day, creativity and resourcefulness are going to be on the wane. It is possible to put in long hours without producing corresponding results. The law of diminishing returns applies to the length of the workday.

High-impact time managers value their leisure and other parts of their nonwork life. Since high-impact time managers use work time so effectively, they have more leisure time and can take better advantage of it. Leisure is valued for itself and for its capacity to refresh and revitalize.

LESSONS OF SUCCESS LEARNED TOO WELL

Achievement is not accidental. Successful people spend much of their lives acquiring and perfecting skills that make them effective at work. As much concentration and discipline is required to climb the career ladder as to become an accomplished musician or chess master. Success skills are learned gradually, but they become second nature. In fact, we become so comfortable with our success skills that we sometimes use them to deal with leisure activities and personal relationships.

As you strive for success, the time spent working tends to increase, intruding into your leisure time and the time that should be devoted to your family or other personal relationships. The sheer amount of time devoted to work tends to crowd out recreation and relationships that are needed to retain a healthy balance between your work life and your personal life.

The problem of a shrinking personal life is compounded by changes in the way we approach nonwork activities and relationships. The success skills learned for our work lives become ingrained habits that tend to spill over into the rest of our lives. However, those task-oriented skills that are so useful at work prove to be detrimental when applied to the enjoyment of leisure and the development of relationships.

Now let's get specific about the career skills that help at work but hinder at home. While many things contribute to career success, a mastery of the following skills and development of the personal characteristics listed are most important:

- Delayed gratification
- Goal setting
- Objectivity in evaluating situations and people
- Planning and scheduling
- Meeting deadlines
- Measuring up to external quotas and standards
- Playing to win
- Emotional self-control

With these skills, an individual is generally able to meet the expectations of the most demanding boss. To the extent that these skills are mastered, a person can develop competence quickly and surely in a variety of jobs. The ability to gain competence in a job quickly puts an energetic person on the fast track.

At the same time you are developing the skills for success, certain other characteristics are being suppressed. As you learn to analyze people and situations objectively, you lose some of your playfulness and impulsiveness. When things are carefully planned, little room is left for spontaneity. When trying to win your point in a heated discussion, you learn to suppress openness and hide your true feelings. Concentrating on task completion discourages the enjoyment of the process or activity that accomplishes the goal. Emotional control and the image of professionalism make expression of genuine feelings almost impossible.

The success skills are important to accomplishment at work, and most of this book has been devoted to helping you develop just such skills. However, when these skills are used as a primary way of dealing with leisure time and personal relationships, your life-style becomes unbalanced. You lose the ability to relax and enjoy yourself. You may take time away from work, but you do not relax. You may even engage in various recreational activities, but you will find that they do not refresh or restore you.

The workaholic has tremendous difficulty with leisure time. If leisure activities are sedentary, such as reading or bird watching, the workaholic generally regards them as a "complete waste of time." Any attempt at such activities will produce great frustration because there is no "output" and no way to keep score.

More robust leisure activities create even more problems for the workaholic. If the workaholic takes up jogging, tennis, or squash, he or she will soon have turned it into a self-improvement project. The object of jogging becomes to see how far and how fast one can run. Soon our workaholic is keeping detailed records of distances run, times, heart rate, and blood pressure. The runner's daily log is more complete and complex than most factory production schedules.

Soon the workaholic jogger is looking for races to run. He or she may start with a "fun run," but will quickly graduate to serious competition. In its full-blown form this competitiveness borrowed from work will result in marathon running.

Under these circumstances, recreational activities are not enjoyed for their own sake. They become a means to an end. It's the competition that counts. The work orientation of goals, persistence, and external evaluation prevails. The career skills work. And they work because the workaholic has turned leisure into another job. Instead of a respite from work, leisure has become simply another job.

If your success skills have contaminated your personal relationships, you will find yourself applying work standards to your personal life. You may feel a distance from those you cherish and find intimacy difficult to establish. You may spend time with those you love but find it difficult to be open, spontaneous, and playful. You will probably find yourself wishing you were alone more of the time.

Your success skills may serve you well at work, but they undermine your ability to use nonwork time in a rich and fulfilling way. Leisure should not be turned into a part-time job as competitive as your normal career. Personal relationships do not grow and develop when subjected to the task completion mentality so important for career achievement. Different approaches and different skills are needed to grow relationships and enjoy leisure.

THE IMPORTANCE OF LEISURE AND RECREATION

Hard-charging workaholics often scoff at those who are less driven. Being too busy to take a vacation is a badge of honor to the workaholic. Yet the work-obsessed person is seldom as productive as the high-impact time manager who effectively balances work, leisure, and personal relationships. Productivity depends much more on what gets done than on the number of hours at work. The high-impact time manager knows how to pack the work hours full of productivity.

Leisure is not a reward for a job well done or time off for good behavior. Recreation should not be another arena in which to demonstrate your competence or prove your competitive superiority. Leisure and recreation are important because they are necessary for health and happiness. Properly pursued, leisure activities reduce stress, strengthen the body, and refresh the mind. The unconscious processes of creativity are nurtured by rest and reflection afforded by leisure time.

Upon retirement, few people say, "Gee, I wish I had spent more time working." On the contrary, they are more likely to complain about too little time spent with family and friends. They will remember soccer games missed and anniversaries celebrated over the telephone because of business trips. They may recall friendships that withered from lack of attention. They also regret the vacations not taken and the hobbies never pursued.

The high-impact time manager creates a balanced life-style. Work is important, and great effort and skill are devoted to developing a career. Leisure is valued, and time is set aside simply to enjoy life. Relationships are cherished, and time is devoted to nurturing love and friendship. The high-impact time manager knows that too little time devoted to any one of these areas of life will eventually produce unhappiness. The trick is achieving balance.

ACHIEVING BALANCE

The first step in achieving a balanced life-style is to make certain that enough time is devoted to your life outside work. In all likelihood you are already working enough hours per week.

As time management consultants, we find few people who need to devote more hours to their work. If anything, they need to work fewer hours but use those hours more effectively.

At first, devoting less time to work may be difficult. This is particularly true if you feel that things are not going well at work. Your natural tendency may be to redouble your efforts at work. But if you are suffering from burnout or if you are a workaholic, the prescription is less time at work—not more.

Initially, you should make small changes and strive for small successes in restoring the balance between work and nonwork. Your hardest challenge in the beginning will be convincing yourself that it is OK to devote time to leisure while there is still work to be done. You may feel guilty taking time for yourself while there is still work to be done. However, your leisure and your relationships cannot wait until all the work is done—because all the work will never be done. This is simply an impossible standard.

Withholding leisure from yourself because of unfinished work is counterproductive as well as unrealistic. By this impossible standard, you would *never* deserve any leisure. When you deny yourself leisure or a meaningful personal life, you have increased your degree of burnout. Burnout, in turn, reduces your ability to use work time effectively. While leisure should be pursued as an end in itself, the work-related benefits of a balanced life-style should be recognized.

People who make good use of the nonwork time are skillful in managing the transitions between work and their life after work. Some people are unable to relax because they are unable to make the transition from work. They may come home, but they are still at work mentally. They may talk to their spouses, but they talk about work and continue to grapple with the day's problems. People who make effective transitions between work and life after work usually have transition routines or rituals.

Jane Lawson, an account executive for a brokerage firm, changes clothes and wears her hair differently after work. These changes allow her to slow the pace of her day and get ready to deal with people in a less competitive manner. Walt Teller, a school teacher, walks through his garden after school, looking at the new growth and pulling a few weeds before going into the house. When he leaves his garden, the cares of the day are left behind, too. These transition times make it possible to change gears mentally and prepare for a new way of relating to people and activities.

Just as there are skills and characteristics that promote effective use of work time, there are attitudes and skills that allow us to make the most of leisure time. Leisure activities should be pursued because they are inherently interesting, fun, or relaxing. They are ends in themselves. You play checkers with your daughter to enjoy her company, not to enjoy a competitive victory. You go jogging for the pleasure of feeling your muscles work and the tension dissipate.

The attitudes and skills needed to benefit from leisure and recreation include

- The willingness to be process oriented instead of product oriented.
- The ability to engage in activities without judging the results in terms of success and failure.
- Openness to sensory experiences.
- Willingness to express yourself freely.
- The ability to flow with experiences.
- The ability to transcend time-consciousness.
- The ability to act spontaneously and impulsively.

As you can see, the attitudes and skills needed to use leisure well are very different from those required for career success. Both sets of skills are needed to live a balanced life-style. Just as important, you need to be able to make the transition between the two sets of skills appropriately.

GETTING IN TOUCH WITH YOUR FEELINGS

Our work roles frequently require us to mask our feelings. When Latham Wagner, a furniture store manager, deals with a dissatisfied customer, he carefully hides any frustration or irritation he may feel. The sales representative who loses an important account may feel like cussing or crying but holds those impulses in check. The supervisor who has to reprimand a chronically late employee may be extremely nervous, but will make every effort to hide the nervousness.

These activities may be referred to as professionalism, presenting the proper image, keeping one's cool, or maintaining objectivity. In any case, all these activities create a disconnection between how we feel and how we behave. Over time this tendency gets stronger and spills over into nonwork activities. Workaholics frequently find themselves out of touch with their feelings. To enjoy and benefit from leisure time, we must be in touch with our feelings.

If you are out of touch with your feelings, special steps may be required to link what you feel with what you do. While it takes time and effort, reestablishing the link between feeling and doing is possible and worthwhile. Here are some suggestions for getting in touch with your feelings:

Suggestion 1: Immerse yourself in a single activity.

In our drive for success, we frequently hurry and try to do several things at once. Hurrying and doubling up on activities means that we are only half paying attention. Truly paying attention to any activity will reveal that it is richer, more subtle, and more complex than expected. Contrast the following approaches to writing a letter.

Jack has been meaning to write to his Army buddy for some time. He decides to write the letter while watching a sitcom on television. He takes his pad and a ballpoint pen into the den and starts to write during the first commercial. He gets the first paragraph started, but the commercials are over and Jack turns his attention back to his program. Before the next set of commercials Jack gets a telephone call but manages to scribble another two sentences during the conversation. Over the course of the next hour, Jack writes while watching television, talking to his wife, and correcting his children. The letter is a little disjointed, but it's finished.

Max also needs to write a letter to an old friend. Max retreats to a quiet room with pen and stationery. Before he starts to write, he takes a few minutes to recall some of the experiences he and his friend have shared. He makes several notes about things he wishes to share in the letter. As Max begins to write he conjures up a mental picture of his friend and begins to smile. Max is pleased by the sound of the pen moving across the page and enjoys the pattern of parallel lines made by his script. As he finishes the letter, Max signs his name with a flourish. The letter flowed and Max was unconcerned about how much time it took or what he was going to do when he finished the letter.

Max's letter may not have been written any better than Jack's, but the activity of writing the letter was richer and more satisfying for Max. For Jack the letter was a task to check off the To Do List; for Max the letter resulted from a pleasant activity which recalled fond memories and added another little bond to an old friendship. Jack was interested in the letter as a product. Max was interested in and fully involved with the *process* that produced the letter.

Suggestion 2: Develop a new interest.

Career-focused people often have little in their lives besides their work. Even when they are not working, the demands and concerns of their jobs are not far from their minds. How you use your time away from work determines whether the time is idleness or leisure. Leisure is time devoted to interesting pursuits or pastimes. These leisure pursuits may be passive, such as listening to music, or active, such as hiking or woodworking. The important feature is that the activity itself provides pleasure and satisfaction.

The range of leisure interests is much larger than generally realized. Possible interests include entertainment, solitude, friendship, community involvement, personal growth, physical activity, spiritual development, social responsibility, and creative expression. A few hours a week devoted to an interest can add both depth and breadth to your life.

Developing an interest outside work does not detract from the seriousness with which you approach your career. Consider the examples to two very serious high achievers. Winston Churchill was an avid painter who found time for this pursuit even when he was enormously busy. Malcolm Forbes, publisher of *Forbes* magazine, is a motorcycle enthusiast who has cycled across the Soviet Union.

Suggestion 3: Be Playful.

Playfulness, especially when combined with a sense of humor, can add tremendously to your sense of well-being. Play is active relaxation in which you become deeply and pleasantly involved. You participate for the fun and enjoyment of the activity instead of the satisfaction of winning.

Play is focused on the activity itself, not on what the outcome of the activity may bring. Competitiveness undermines play. This is particularly hard to remember when it comes to "playing" games. A playful approach to games means that you don't go for the jugular, you don't gloat when you win, and you don't pout when you lose. Play is casual and easygoing. Unless you are able to relax as you play, you will not find it renewing.

Suggestion 4: Develop your sensory awareness.

You probably use your sight fairly well. After all, you rely on your eyes to get you to work, to read the paper, and to watch ball games. Chances are you have neglected your other senses. One of the best ways to begin to get in touch with your feelings is to become open to your senses.

Try the following exercise. Go to your back yard or to a nearby park and pick a comfortable place to sit. Close your eyes and breathe deeply. With your eyes still closed, begin to pay attention to what you hear. Do you hear passing traffic and perhaps some other people enjoying the outdoors? Continue to listen. Do you hear the wind? Do you hear a garbage truck, trains, tug boats, or factory noises? What about animals? Even in an urban environment there are probably birds to be heard.

As you listen, remind yourself that you have probably been shutting out these sounds that tie you to your world. If you are like most of us, you have forgotten how complex and *interesting* your audio world is.

Next notice the temperature. Are you warm or cold? Is it humid? Stretch your hands out and feel where you are sitting. If you are on a bench, feel the texture of the bench. If you are sitting on the ground, use your hand to feel the area immediately around you. Notice the softness of the grass or the texture of the soil, or the grittiness of the gravel, or the solidness of the concrete. Pay attention to the smells around you. Is the air fresh or does it smell of smog? Are there any flowers in bloom to add their scent to the air? Can you smell how *you* smell? Now try taste. First, notice how your mouth tastes at the moment. Can you taste your last cup of coffee or the candy bar you ate at break time?

This sensory awareness exercise should help you shift gears from your career focus. Unless you have performed this exercise in a park where you are afraid of being mugged, you should find it relaxing. When you pay attention to the information available from your senses, you cannot resist temporarily letting go of your task orientation. As you set aside your work skills, you begin to feel. And feeling makes free time relaxing and relationships rewarding.

BUILDING STRONGER RELATIONSHIPS

Try an experiment. Talk with some people who are retired about the things that meant the most to them in their lives. Ask them what are the most important things to them today. You will occasionally find someone who talks about career achievements or how much money they have made. More often you may hear about the importance of health. However, the most common theme will be the importance of relationships.

Some will tell you how important their spouses have been to them. Others will talk about their children. Their relationships with their children may be sources of pride or dismay, but seldom are they indifferent to the relationship. Still others will tell you about the importance of that one long-term friend. In any case, a balanced life-style requires meaningful relationships. The following suggestions should help to foster relationships.

Suggestion 1: Devote time to building and maintaining relationships.

The quality of a relationship depends on a number of factors. However, the most important factor is time. Time is required to begin a relationship. Relationships are built on mutual interests, mutual respect, and mutual trusts. None of these can be established without spending time together.

This is dramatically illustrated at the beginning of most romantic relationships. Enormous amounts of time and energy are devoted to thinking about the relationship, planning for the time to be spent together, preparing to spend time together, and paying attention to each other's needs while together. Early in romantic relationships each person makes a special effort to set time aside to devote exclusively to the other person. They may be able to spend hours alone just talking and resent the interruption of anyone or anything else.

The sheer amount of time invested in a relationship is important. If two people spend little time together, their investment in the relationship will be so small that neither of them is likely to value it highly. While this is obviously true when a relationship is in its formative stages, it is equally true of a long-term relationship. If people spend little time together, they cease to know each other in a deep way.

Suggestion 2: Invest "Quality Time" in your relationships.

The advice to spend "quality time" with those who are important to you is almost a cliche. Yet the advice is sound. As we pointed out when discussing work, it is not the number of hours as much as it is how the hours are used.

To build or maintain a relationship, you have to have time in which to provide undivided attention to the other person in the relationship. Undivided attention sends the message that the other person is valued. A friend of ours, a psychologist, makes certain that he takes his nine-year-old son on two backpacking camping trips a year. On this particular type of outing, the two are alone together for a minimum of three days. The son, Brandon, does not have to compete with his father's patients, his sister, or his mother for his father's attention on these trips.

It is extremely important for couples with kids to learn to give each other quality time. For couples, quality time is not sitting in the same room silently watching television. Quality time is paying attention to the other person on an intellectual, emotional, and physical level.

Suggestion 3: Create intimacy.

Discussing intimacy makes many people uncomfortable. Intimacy is regarded as a private matter, and many hard-boiled, hard-driving achievers would refuse to discuss such issues. Yet almost everyone hungers for intimacy, whether they are willing to talk about it or not. Achieving and maintaining an intimate relationship is a subtle art, but closeness and nurturing inherent in such relationships make the required efforts worthwhile.

The skills required to develop and maintain intimacy are complex, but there are some rather straightforward ways of promoting intimacy. These include

1. Showing thoughtfulness.
2. Open communications.
3. Periods of undivided attention.
4. Preservation of confidences.
5. Sharing small pleasures.
6. Developing a "shared heritage."
7. Creating a little romance.

If you build these seven characteristics into your approach to personal relationships, the degree of intimacy will grow. If you are not as emotionally close as you once were, it is quite likely you can repair the damage and foster greater intimacy. While it will take time, it may be the most important thing you do.

CONCLUSION

High achievers frequently have difficulty attaining a balanced life-style. The very skills they found so valuable in achieving work-related goals actually hinder them in their nonwork lives. They are often unable to relax and find it increasingly difficult to maintain healthy personal relationships.

The first step for achieving balance is to realize that success hasn't brought all the happiness expected. The second step is to realize that career skills are inappropriate for leisure and personal relationships. The skills for leisure and personal relationships must be learned (or relearned).

A balanced life-style is the aim of effective time management. High-impact time management makes it possible to be effective at work while still having the time for leisure and personal relationships.

CHAPTER 7

How to Give Up Fire Fighting Forever

Henry Mintzberg, one of our keenest observers of executive life, reminds us of the hectic and disjointed nature of the managerial workday. During a typical workday, most activities last only a few minutes and end with an interruption. Consequently, it is necessary to pick up many partially completed activities in midstream and get them finished.

The pace tends to be quick and the unexpected demands relentless. The normal pattern of the managerial workday encourages a "fire-fighting" approach to management. The fire-fighting approach to management sees the world as one crisis after another. Some of the crises are huge, but most of them are small, garden-variety crises. Both types of crises work against planned and measured responses to challenging situations. Most managers operating in the fire-fighting mode are convinced that they have no other alternative. However, such is not the case.

Important problems that could not possibly be anticipated or prevented do arise with some frequency. These problems, of course, must be addressed with speed and flexibility. However, those addicted to crisis management styles of operation use these inevitable crises to excuse their own lack of foresight and planning. The fire fighter seems to create crises where none should exist.

HOW TO CREATE A CRISIS ATMOSPHERE

Consider the case of Elmore Whittelson. Elmore is a risk manager for a large utility company providing electric power to several hundred thousand customers. His job is to examine the company's operations for possible risks and minimize the company's exposure to such risks.

Utility companies face numerous risks in the areas of employee health and safety, public safety, and possible damage to property and equipment. Mr. Whittelson's department has to deal with the trivial and the potentially catastrophic.

On the trivial end of the spectrum, his department has to

decide whether or not the company will take responsibility for replacing shrubs that a customer believes were destroyed by the company's installation of an underground cable. On the other end of the spectrum, the department has responsibility for planning emergency evacuation of the 20 square miles surrounding the company's nuclear power plant in case of a meltdown.

Some of these problems are routine and predictable. These would include developing safety and customer service programs for the installers who deal with the commercial and residential customers. Dealing with these issues should be relatively simple and straightforward.

When a tornado tears through the area, the risk manager's problems are anything but routine. Service is interrupted, live power lines may be down, and factories and offices may have to close. Even more serious is the threat to essential community services such as police protection, fire protection, and medical services. Since the timing of such emergencies cannot be predicted, quick and resourceful responses are essential.

Crisis management is appropriate in a situation where it is not possible to prevent or predict the problem. However, most people prone to crisis management invent their own crises by turning garden-variety problems into adrenaline-pumping emergencies. Whittelson, our utility company risk manager, is one such person. Let's look at how he handled what should have been a routine project assigned by his boss.

Whittelson's boss, Roger Dasston, has asked him to devise a new customer service training program for the company's residential installers. The program's objectives, according to Dasston, are to improve the impression installers make on customers and reduce the likelihood that the installers will do anything that might put the company at risk. According to the program plan, classroom sessions are to be supplemented with role-playing exercises, and a video cassette is to be given to each installer. A test needs to be devised to evaluate how much the installers will have learned from the program.

Dasston made the assignment during the first week in March. The kickoff date for the first class of installer was set for September 4. This timetable gave Whittelson six months to design the program, prepare instructional materials, and obtain appropriate instructors for the courses. Six months is ample time for putting together such a program, but the time is tight enough to require close adherence to a carefully designed schedule.

For the first three months Whittelson does nothing on the project. The first week in June he asks his summer intern from a local college to start collecting materials on customer service programs used by other companies.

Three days later, his intern returns with about 15 photocopied articles describing customer service programs in various kinds of organizations. He also has brochures from a number of companies that custom design programs and conduct training. He also has brochures from companies that sell various kinds of training materials off the shelf.

Whittelson thanks his intern and stacks the material on top of a filing cabinet so that it will be conveniently available when he finds some time to study it. There it sits for another three weeks until Mr. Dasston asks Whittelson how he is doing on the project.

Whittelson responds, "Fine, fine—making excellent progress. Got my college kid working on it. I'll have some stuff to show you next week." At this point the adrenaline starts to flow, but just a little.

So Whittelson begins to look for the material his student intern dug up. It takes him about 20 minutes to find the materials. In the meantime, he has put out an all-points bulletin for his intern.

By the time the intern rushes apprehensively into Whittelson's office, the materials have been found. Whittelson spends much of the remainder of the afternoon going through the material. For the first time he realizes just how time consuming this project will be.

He leaves for home that afternoon with a tiny knot in his stomach, a knot put there by the realization that he has done virtually nothing on a rather large project that must be completed in less than two months. He ruefully notes that two-thirds of the time allotted for the project has slipped by. No one to blame but himself, he thinks, as he heads out of the parking lot.

Whittelson intends to get started on the project the next day, but several unexpected things keep him distracted for the better part of a week. When he does get started on planning the project Thursday afternoon, he realizes the he had better find some video production facilities and begin writing a script. He also makes a note to find out if he needs to hire some actors for the video or if he can use some of the people in the company. He makes another note that an instructor for the class needs to be hired.

The next six weeks are extremely hectic. Whittelson and his intern devote almost full time to preparing the materials for the customer service training program. Everything is done hurriedly, and they have to pay "rush" charges for some of the typesetting and printing. The in-house television studio is already booked solid, forcing Whittelson to pay premium prices for an outside video production company.

The materials are done just hours before the first class is to meet. Unable to find an instructor at the last minute, Whittelson decides to teach the first round of classes himself. Other projects are put on the back burner while he prepares for his course.

What's the problem here? Why has Whittelson put himself under such strain? Why has he risked public embarrassment by letting things slide so long that he barely had time to complete the project? The puzzling answer is that Whittelson finds this approach extremely rewarding.

THE REWARDS OF CRISIS MANAGEMENT

Whittelson's approach to his customer service project provided him with a lot of rewards that are difficult to recognize at first. Even Whittelson is not aware of many of these rewards. But rewards they are, and he relishes them. Let's take a look at a few of these rewards for crisis management.

People who are in the midst of a crisis get a lot of attention. During the last month before the customer service program was to begin, everyone on his floor knew that Whittelson was coming in early and leaving late, pulling out all the stops to make the deadline. This got him a lot of attention, and getting attention can be a pleasant reward.

People who are dealing with a crisis tend to feel important. After all, they are saving the company from a disaster, or at least a major embarrassment. Only an important person would have that capability, right? Never mind that they created the crisis.

Working against a serious deadline with the outcome in

doubt is exciting. The adrenaline really does flow. Adrenaline is a powerful chemical stimulant produced by the body to provide extra energy for "fight or flight" in emergencies. Many people find the stimulation provided by adrenaline very satisfying. When their lives are not naturally exciting enough, some people tend to engineer situations that will produce crises.

Generating a crisis is also a way of defying authority. Most people know that projects such as the one just described would go more smoothly if they were carefully mapped out in advance and accomplished in an orderly, one-step-at-a-time fashion. Even big projects can be accomplished with relatively little fuss if they are approached systematically over a reasonable period of time. This is the way most bosses prefer things done.

The crisis maker is anything but orderly and systematic. The normal pattern is a long period of procrastination followed by frenzied efforts to salvage the project. This pattern of behavior is an excellent way to defy the boss's authority. It is also a fairly safe way to be defiant. The rebellion is indirect and the motives are concealed.

The crisis maker is frequently a person who is bored relatively easily and has a high need for stimulation. When work isn't exciting enough, he or she simply manufactures a crisis. Guess what? The job is no longer boring.

Unfortunately, our stimulation junkie creates excitement for other people as well. Our crisis maker rushes around, commandeering people and resources to meet the crisis, and other people are caught up in the problems (real or imagined) of the crisis. They drop the work they are doing to help resolve the crisis or just to watch the drama unfold.

In either case, they are neglecting their own priorities. Our stress junkie's need for an adrenaline fix has created an unnecessary uproar. Our crisis maker's need for stimulation generates anxiety and disorder throughout the organization. The results for the productivity of co-workers and the organization are anything but healthy.

DEALING WITH A CRISIS MAKER

Most of us have to deal with at least one stimulation junkie or crisis maker. It may be the boss or it may be some family member. Learning to deal effectively with a crisis maker can significantly reduce the amount of frustration you experience on a daily basis.

The first step is to identify the problem. Who are the people in your life who tend to create crises? Does your boss always have to rush on things that should be handled with ease? Do you have a subordinate who is always late with reports? Do you have a colleague who seems to have endless excuses for arriving late to meetings? These behaviors make them suspects for the role of crisis maker. Just recognizing the problem for what it is gives you certain advantages.

When you have identified a person as a crisis maker or a stress junkie, you have new information that will help you respond more appropriately to the chaos and disorder created by the person. This new insight can help you change your perspective:

Insight 1: Since the crisis is "manufactured," its importance and urgency are probably less than the crisis maker would have us believe.

This insight will help you to resist being caught up in the crisis. You can be more level-headed about your decision to help resolve the crisis. Instead of relying on the crisis maker's sense of panic to gauge the importance of the problems faced, you can calmly assess the situation with a healthy dose of skepticism.

Insight 2: You do not have to share the emotions of the crisis maker.

Whether or not you decide to become involved in solving the problems associated with the crisis, you can decide not to become as emotionally charged up as the crisis maker. Controlling your emotions in a situation such as this lets you keep a more objective perspective. With this perspective, you are less likely to set your own priorities aside to rescue the crisis maker.

Insight 3: You can make your own plans that take the crisis maker's tendencies into account.

If your boss has a tendency to do everything in a last-minute rush, it is difficult not to get caught up in the cycle.

However, it is possible to get out in front of the crisis maker. If you are going to have a role in resolving the crisis, find out what that is going to be early. Don't wait for the boss to catch you at the last minute.

Anticipate or ask what will be needed from you. Then proceed to finish your part of the project ahead of time. When the boss rushes in at the last minute, your contribution is already prepared. You will have successfully transformed your portion of the crisis into a routine task.

Insight 4: Fire Fighting is an expensive way to get things done.

Fire fighters frequently put in long hours and expend enormous amounts of energy. If they are managers or professionals who are not paid overtime, it may appear that the organization is getting a bargain. Such is seldom the case.

Fire fighting wastes resources. To meet crisis-created deadlines, other people have to work extra hours as well, and many of these people will have to be paid overtime. A crisis also may require calling in outside contractors or hiring temporary help. On top of all this, the routine business of the organization suffers during a crisis, while other important, but not urgent, projects are completely ignored. The final cost is the emotional exhaustion of the people involved in responding to the crisis.

Insight 5: You don't have to reward "fire fighting" or crisis management.

One of the big rewards of fire fighting is that it makes the fire fighter or crises manager something of a hero. If an important project is put together at the last minute with heroic efforts on the part of the crisis manager, praise for extra effort is often forthcoming. This praise simply reinforces fire fighting.

This insight warns you against providing praise or other rewards for destructive behavior. If you are dealing with a subordinate or a co-worker, you might point out that this project did not have to be a crisis in the first place. You might also indicate that you will be much more responsive to requests for assistance that come early in the process.

WHEN *YOU* ARE THE CRISIS MAKER

A bigger problem exists if you are one of the crisis makers and fire fighters in your organization. First, you have to admit that you cause your own problems—always a difficult task. Second, you have to devise tactics that undercut your regular, long-standing, habitual ways of dealing with situations. This type of change is difficult.

The rewards for change can be even greater than the rewards for fire fighting and crisis management. High achievers generally operate at a fast pace, but they have learned to give up fire fighting. The rewards of giving up fire fighting include

- **An enhanced reputation for reliability.** When everything is a crisis, you inevitably drop the ball from time to time. When you give up the joys of fire fighting, you tend to bring projects in on time with little fuss or hassle. Over the long haul, a reputation for reliability will serve you better than will a reputation for making extraordinary efforts in lost causes.
- **More support from your colleagues when you encounter a real emergency.** The story of the boy who cried wolf applies here. If your life and your work is a constant crisis, people learn to play down the importance of your claims and demands. If you have to ask for help less frequently, you are more likely to receive it when needed.
- **Improvement of your mental and physical health.** While stress junkies enjoy their adrenaline rushes, living under that kind of pressure promotes a number of stress-related disorders that can permanently damage your health.
- **Developing a reputation for competence.** Few characteristics are more admired than competence. Proven competence is the currency of continuing achievement and success. This is a reputation worth building and protecting.

If you are a fire fighter, it is because you choose to be. You are equally free to give up fire fighting. While it is not easy to make significant changes in well-established habits, it is possible. Here are some tips to help you give up fire fighting and crisis management.

Tactic 1: Respond to a large project by devising a detailed schedule for its completion.

One of the biggest problems fire fighters have is getting started. They tend to procrastinate as long as there is sufficient time to get the project completed without a hassle. A schedule shared with the boss and frequently reviewed with the boss can overcome much of this early procrastination.

Tactic 2: Plan your work and work from your plan.

Most fire fighters do not use a daily plan to guide their activities throughout the day. They are reactive people who are extremely responsive to the most pressing demand of the moment. They may have calendars and To Do Lists, but they seldom follow them. However, it is almost impossible to break the fire-fighting habit without the self-discipline to devise a plan and stick to it.

Tactic 3: Substitute small, insignificant crises for large, threatening ones.

Crisis makers enjoy the excitement and stimulation that comes from a crisis. If you are a crisis maker, you may find your job rather boring unless there is a crisis. If this is the case, go ahead and create crises, but create small, useful ones that are not so hard on you and everyone around you.

Take that big project that you are procrastinating on and divide it up into small increments. Make the accomplishment of each increment a goal, setting an almost impossible deadline. Proceed as you normally would on one particular increment. Get some other people involved in some of these small subprojects. Create a crisis atmosphere and enjoy yourself.

You have substituted a number of small crises for one large one. These small crises are much less draining on your colleagues, and they help to prevent large crises by allowing you to complete your project on time.

Tactic 4: Empower other people to help you prevent crisis management.

Your friends, family, and associates can assist you in overcoming your tendency to embroil yourself in crises. You can empower them to assist you. Discuss these tendencies frankly with people who have your best interests at heart. Ask them to warn you when they see you about to take action that will create a crisis. Even more important, have them warn you when they notice you neglecting responsibilities in a way that will inevitably lead to a crisis.

Tactic 5: Make all urgent matters pass the "Importance Test."

You are probably attracted to urgent tasks. They are probably more fun and interesting than your routine work. Urgent tasks are great excuses for avoiding unpleasant tasks. Recognize this attraction and its potential for distracting you from your priorities.

When an urgent task or an emerging crisis presents itself, make it pass the Importance Test before you devote any real time to it. Unless you can determine that this urgent problem is more important than the things already on your To Do List, you should ignore it.

You also need to ask the question, "Important to whom?" While it is likely that the people presenting their problems to you will believe that nothing should take greater priority, that is not the relevant consideration. You need to determine how important the crisis is to the effectiveness of the organization. Then you can decide whether your time should be diverted from your planned activities.

Tactic 6: Add more outside activities to your agenda to increase your overall level of stimulation.

Adding more variety to your activities will increase the level of stimulation you receive. If you have a number of interesting and unusual outside activities, you are less likely to need to generate turmoil at work. Volunteer to work a few hours in a nursing home, run for the city council, or begin collecting Civil War documents.

Tactic 7: Plan some variety into your day at work.

As you plan your daily schedule, be certain to include a variety of activities. This will reduce the likelihood of boredom and provide some needed stimulation. If you have to write a report in the morning, make certain that you plan something that will take you away from your desk in the afternoon. Perhaps you could balance the report writing with a visit to a client who needs to see you or with some other work that would be a change of pace.

Tactic 8: Increase the amount of time you spend with people outside work.

An active family and social life provides stimulation and a balance to work. Set time aside to participate in family or social life. Provide yourself with time to loaf and with time for active, structured recreation.

Tactic 9: Take up a hobby or sport that uses very different skills from those you use on the job.

The range of skills required for most jobs is relatively small. Executives need to have strong analytical skills and even stronger people skills. Physicians need very strong scientific and diagnostic skills. A dentist needs excellent hand-eye coordination. A building contractor needs to be able to deal with a wide variety of people and juggle many responsibilities simultaneously.

People in each of these occupations need to pick hobbies or other recreational pursuits that involve skills other than those they have honed on the job. Developing pursuits that diverge from occupational interests provides a needed separation between work and leisure. It also provides a stimulation that may be missing at work.

These tips to overcome fire fighting can provide important guidance in charting a better way to manage your time. On occasion you will fall back into the habit of approaching even routine problems in a crisis mode. When this happens, remind yourself of how destructive this habit can be. Also review the rewards for avoiding crises.

A FINAL WORD ON FIRE FIGHTING

This chapter has been devoted to overcoming the tendency to create crises and respond to situations as if you were fighting fires. This is sound advice that will improve both your effectiveness and your peace of mind. However, we do not want to leave the impression that it is *never* appropriate to deal with a crisis in a fire-fighting manner.

At times, events can overwhelm the best laid plans. Your competitor comes out with a revolutionary product that makes your bread and butter product line obsolete. Obviously, this is a real emergency that threatens the survival of your company. A new product line must be developed as soon as possible. Crisis management is highly appropriate in this situation.

Just save your fire-fighting skills for a real fire.

CHAPTER 8

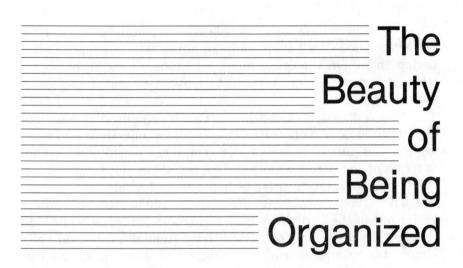

The
Beauty
of
Being
Organized

We know a number of people who are quite disorganized. In fact, we could call them slobs in public without fear of slandering them. On the other hand, we know a handful of people who are impeccably organized. We leave it to you to pick your own category.

The contrast and conflict between organized people and disorganized people plays itself out in all organizations and most families. Organized people always claim the moral high ground in terms of competence and efficiency, and the slobs have to settle for the consolation prize of being more lovable.

These contrasts were delightfully illustrated in endless variations in the Broadway play and television series "The Odd Couple." In the television series, Tony Randall portrayed Felix Unger, the quintessential "neatnik," and Jack Klugman was masterful as Oscar Madison, the complete slob. The show's popularity was in part a reflection of the audience's recognition of a kernel of truth in these two stereotypes.

While Oscar may have some appealing characteristics, this chapter is devoted to showing you how to adopt some of Felix's neatnik tricks. Being organized is a beautiful thing. It means never having to say "I can't find it." Being organized can give you a sense of calm and confidence that translates into accomplishment.

THE SERIOUS TOOLS
OF A WELL-ORGANIZED PERSON

Getting organized is serious business that requires serious tools. However, the very serious tools of a well-organized person are surprisingly simple and commonplace. They consist of

- A desk
- A calendar

- A set of files
- A daily time log

All organized people use these tools or some variation of them. The power of these tools to create order and promote accomplishment are greatly underestimated, perhaps because of their very simplicity. Equally confusing is the fact that many disorganized people also use these tools.

The real difference is that organized people know how to use each and every one of these simple tools to produce a high-impact performance. When these tools are used effectively, little time is wasted, and every hour produces results. We shall take a fresh look at each of these tools, exploring the best way to use each one as a time management and organization tool.

THE DESK

You have been using your desk so long that you take it for granted. Now we are going to point out how you should and should not use your desk. You may appropriately use your desk as

- A writing surface.
- A reading surface.
- A place to sort materials needed for various tasks and projects.
- A place to store work materials.
- A place to file frequently used materials.
- The location of an in-basket for collecting work that should be attended to immediately.
- The location of an out-basket for collecting completed work to be filed or sent forward.

It is inappropriate to use your desk for

- Stacking papers randomly.
- Storing magazines and newspaper you plan to read "sometime."

- Stacking books you have used but haven't gotten around to returning to the library or your bookshelf.
- Aging printouts of last year's inventory.
- Storing enough food to last you through the next ice age.
- Storing unopened mail from last year.

Upon reflection, you will probably regard our list of misuses for a desk as rather pedestrian and uncreative. You may have a few originals that would make ours pale by comparison, but you get the point. Most people use their desks to do plenty of things other than useful work. Some people have so much junk on their desks that they cannot use them for *any* meaningful work.

We have several very disorganized friends who carry the messy desk syndrome to an extreme. One is a college professor who never seems to remove anything from his desk during the course of an academic year. Near the end of the year he begins to cover his floor as well as his desk. Each May, however, he cleans his office, throwing away mountains of paper. One year he piled all the trash in a four-foot heap in the hall in front of his office door. Then put the following sign on the door:

Housekeeper,
Please vacuum the floor today.
It may be your last chance for a year.
Thanks.

A similarly sloppy colleague keeps his desk stacked so high that it is impossible for him to write at his desk. He solved this problem by obtaining a key to a vacant office down the hall. He goes there to write reports, answer correspondence, or sort materials of any kind. As you might expect, the desk in the spare office is beginning to get that familiar cluttered look as well. Since there are no more empty offices, who knows how he will cope when the "vacant" office also overflows with paper and other clutter.

We are not recommending that you keep a perfectly clean

desk. Harold Geneen, former chairman and CEO of ITT, claimed that the only person with a clean desk is someone who isn't doing anything. He has a point. A busy person working on a variety of tasks during any given day is likely to have a number of things scattered about the desk. However, the things on a well-organized person's desk will pertain to *current* projects.

The well-organized person makes a habit putting things away when they are no longer needed. The well-organized person will also know *where* a given item should be put away. These people really believe that there should be "a place for everything and everything should be in its place." But more about that when we discuss filing systems.

Here are some tips for making the best use of your desk:

Tip 1: At the end of the day, remove as many items as possible from the top of your desk.

When you start work the next day, you won't be distracted by the clutter from the day before. This should help you get a quick start. This will also reduce the number of items misplaced or lost.

Tip 2: Use an in-basket and an out-basket to keep current work separated from completed work and tasks not yet tackled.

Clutter is distracting. If your desk is a jumble of papers, you will find it difficult to concentrate on the job at hand. An in-basket conveniently holds work that needs to be done today without allowing it to spill over onto the desk and contribute to clutter. Similarly, an out-basket groups together pieces of paper that have already been processed. All that should remain on the desk top are papers relevant to your current project. Such a procedure allows you to focus your attention and improve your concentration.

Tip 3: Store equipment such as your scissors, stapler, and tape in a desk drawer.

Almost every desk is equipped with these or similar items. They take up space on the top of the desk but are used relatively infrequently. Stored in a desk drawer, they are readily available, but do not add to the messiness of the desk.

> Tip 4: Position your desk within your office so that you find it pleasant and comfortable to spend time sitting there.

If you work in an office, you will probably spend more time sitting at your desk than doing anything else. Consequently, you need to be comfortable. Some people need their desks turned toward the window. Others find it easier to work if their desks face the door so they can see and respond to approaching co-workers. Remember, comfort counts.

A CALENDAR

A calendar is an essential tool for anyone who wants to get organized and stay organized. You will be using this tool every day, so be certain you pick one that suits your needs.

Calendars come in a wide variety of styles. There are monthly pocket calendars that show you one day at a time. There are desk calendars bound as books that show a week or a month at a time. There are wall calendars that lay out an entire year on a single piece of paper. There are monthly desk calendars that take the form of ink blotters. The variations on these styles are almost endless.

Picking the right calendar for you and your work pattern is a trial and error process. Coming up with the right calendar or, more likely, set of calendars requires an analysis of your work patterns and some experimentation. You may need to try several different calendars before you find the one that works best.

Your calendar is not to be confused with your To Do List. The two are used in conjunction, but they are not substitutes for each other. A well-kept calendar is an essential input for a meaningful To Do List. The relationship between the two is discussed next.

Some people find that a daily appointment calendar works best for them. Consider the pattern of a dentist's work day. The unit of work is a patient visit. The dentist's day is composed primarily of appointments of varying but predictable lengths.

A dentist works in a single location with patients coming to the office. He or she also has meetings that need to be scheduled from time to time. The best type of calendar for this situation shows one day per page with time marked in 15-minute blocks.

A friend of ours is a sales trainer and seminar leader who works with a variety of clients all over the country. He uses a large, elaborate wall calender showing an entire year at once. He uses different colored magnetic strips to show how many days various trips last. This is an essential tool for booking speaking engagements and reminding his office staff where he will be on any given day of the year.

Most people find that they need at least two calendars. One calendar should serve as a master calendar and remain in one location. For most people the master calendar should be in their office. The second one should be a smaller calendar that can be carried in a pocket or purse. If you monitor complex projects, you may need additional calendars such as the wall calendar just described.

Your master calendar needs to contain everything relevant to job-related scheduling. It should list all the meetings you have to attend and show the estimated time of those meetings. It should list all your appointments, the location of those appointments, and the length of the appointment. Deadlines, milestones, and follow-up dates should be listed. Events that you should know about but not necessarily attend should also be listed. In short, everything of importance to your work life should show up on your master calendar.

Your other calendar should be readily portable. It should be convenient for you to take to meetings and carry on trips. Your personal calendar should be within easy reach throughout your workday. It is one tool you cannot get through the day without. Personal business should be scheduled in your personal calendar.

Your calendar plays a crucial role in getting you organized and keeping you organized. The following tips should help you make your best use of them.

Tip 1: Update all your calendars on a daily basis.

Your calendars are useful only to the extent that they agree with each other. If something gets added to your master calendar, it should show up in your personal calendar. If you make an appointment while at a meeting, you should add it to your personal calendar and transfer it to your master calendar before the day is over. At the beginning of each day, you should check your master calendar against the personal calendar, updating as required.

Tip 2: Provide relevant information when logging an appointment or event on the calendar.

If you are scheduling an appointment for someone to come to your office, be certain to provide enough information to get prepared for the appointment. In addition to the person's name, list telephone number, topic of the meeting, and approximate length of the appointment. This will make it possible to prepare for the meeting. The telephone number is particularly important if the appointment should need to be rescheduled. Writing the number down when the appointment is made can save a scramble for the number later.

Tip 3: If you work with a secretary or an assistant, establish some guidelines for scheduling events on the calendar.

If someone else helps you keep your calendar, develop some guidelines for scheduling. Think about your work patterns. Are there things that have to be done at particular times of the day? What are your high-energy, peak efficiency hours?

One manager we know has a difficult time with Monday mornings. She and her secretary have a standing agreement: no appointments before 11:00 A.M. on Mondays. Another friend who is a "morning person" makes every effort to schedule important meetings before lunch.

Tip 4: Review your calendar at the end of each week.

Examine your calendar at the end of each week. Look at the pattern of time use shown in your calendar. Did you book things too tightly? Did you underestimate the amount of time it would take to accomplish certain tasks? Are activities scheduled throughout the day in accordance with your hours of peak efficiency? In other words, have you scheduled the tasks that require alertness and concentration during your hours of peak efficiency?

Look at the week and the month that are ahead. Does the schedule make good use of your time? Are peak efficiency hours put to good use? Do you need to do any special preparation to meet the demands of the upcoming week? Are there any appointments or events that should be rescheduled?

ORGANIZING YOUR FILES

If your desk is a foot deep in paper, it is probably because your filing system and your mind operate on different organizing principles. Most people clutter up their offices and their homes because they are afraid of being unable to find something important. This is an interesting paradox.

Clutter makers are afraid to throw anything away. They live in fear of needing something that is permanently unavailable. While it might be difficult to find something in the midst of clutter, there is something very comforting about knowing that whatever you are looking for *has* to be around here somewhere. And if you never throw anything away, whatever you are looking for has to be here *somewhere*. It may take you a while to find it, but it can't have disappeared.

The clutter makers fool themselves into believing that the clutter makes no real difference in their effectiveness. They subscribe to the myth that there really is order in the apparent chaos. While no one else may be able to make heads or tails of the mess on their desks, they believe they can find whatever they need with little trouble. Such is just not the case, however.

People who create clutter seem to use the proximity principle for dealing with paper. They want to be able to see the things they need to be working on. The closer the paper is to their work space, the better. A stack of papers on the desk is preferable to a stack on the credenza. Both are better than things filed away out of sight. The clutter makers fear that the maxim about "out of sight, out of mind" is really true.

The organizing principle for most clutter makers is "I need it where I can get to it easily." Where is it more readily available than on the top of the desk? There is a fear that once a piece of paper is filed away, it will be forgotten and appropriate action will not be taken. Worse yet, it may be remembered but it can't be located in the files. The worst fear of all is that the piece of paper will be discarded—permanently lost—when desperately needed.

A new organizing principle is needed, one based on efficiency and convenience. Your new organizing principle should be

Handle it, file it, or throw it away.

This is an organizing principle that is simple but revolutionary. If you do one of these three things with every piece of paper that comes your way, your desk will never again look like the aftermath of a ticker tape parade. Even more important, you will rarely have trouble finding the things you need when you need them.

You need a filing system that is responsive to the way you think and operate. If you are the type of person who thinks in terms of projects, you should have your files organized primarily by projects. If you have an excellent memory for names and consider transactions with people your primary unit of business, you may want to organize your files by people's names. Whatever organizing principle you use, the litmus test is your ability to file something and be able to find it quickly and easily when you need it.

If you have problems with stacks of papers at work, chances are you have similar problems at home. The following tips should help to reduce clutter and restore order in both places.

Tip 1: Establish a tickler file.

A tickler file is a series of 31 file folders numbered from 1 to 31. Each folder represents a day of the month and is used to accumulate pieces of paper to be dealt with on that particular day. If a paper requiring some action cannot be handled on the spot, it should be filed in the tickler file according to the day you plan to handle the item.

The tickler file is really an inventory system for storing paperwork to be done later. If an item has been placed in the tickler file, it is not lost and it is not cluttering up the surface of your desk. You have the comfort of knowing that that particular piece of paper will be handled at an appropriate time. Used consistently, your tickler file becomes a major source of items for your To Do List.

Tip 2: Handle each piece of paper one time only.

This is the tip that makes the new organizing principle work. While some pieces of paper inevitably have to be handled more than once, every effort should be made to minimize the number of times any given piece of paper must pass through your hands.

Most of the clutter on any desk consists of papers examined but not acted upon. Perhaps not enough information was available to make a decision. Perhaps there was not enough time to respond adequately. Or perhaps old-fashioned procrastination is to blame. In any case, most of the paper on the desk has been shuffled but not handled.

A much better approach is to take immediate action as soon as you see the paper the first time. In about 90 percent of the cases, you will have both sufficient time and information to handle the paper immediately. When you really can't respond immediately, file the piece of paper in your tickler file according to the day you will act on it.

Some pieces of paper do not require any action. Your birth certificate is an important piece of paper. However, it requires no action when you receive it from the state Bureau of Vital Statistics. You simply need to file it away so that it is available when you need it. This is the type of paper that should be routinely filed, consuming little of your mind's attention or your desk's surface.

The very best way to dispatch a piece of paper is to throw it away. Scrutinize every piece of paper that crosses your desk. Ask yourself, "What is the worst thing that could happen if I threw this piece of paper away?" If the answer is "not very much," rid yourself of it.

Tip 3: Deal with all your mail the day you receive it.

The mail can be a simple task or an overwhelming burden, depending on your approach to it. Handling today's mail all at once makes it a simple chore. Dragging the chore out during the day increases the likelihood that not all the mail will be handled before the day is over. When this happens, unanswered mail piles up and quickly becomes intimidating.

Be ruthless in applying your organizing principle to the mail. *Answer it, file it, or throw it away.* Much of your mail is junk mail and needs to see a waste basket immediately. Some of your mail consists of announcements or information that can simply be filed. A relatively small part of your mail requires serious action. If you have received a letter that needs a personal reply, write the reply as soon as you have finished reading the letter. Do not let any piece of correspondence fall into the following category: I'll decide if I want to respond later. Items that frequently fall into this category include

- Requests to complete surveys.
- Sales brochures for trips you might want to take.
- Solicitations for subscriptions to magazines.
- Requests for contributions to charities.

When you encounter information on things you would like to do but probably never will do, *make a decision.* Call a travel agent about taking that trip to Aruba, or throw the brochure away. But don't let that piece of paper clutter up your desk.

USING A DAILY TIME LOG

Do you suffer from the scraps of paper syndrome? If so, you find yourself writing notes to yourself on little scraps of paper. Look in your pocket, or your top desk drawer, or under the blotter on your desk. You will probably find some cryptic notes to yourself. If you have the habit of taking notes this way, you probably have at least one horror story about losing an extremely important scrap of paper.

Other people use yellow legal pads in much the same way. They carry the pad around to meetings to make notes. In some offices it is possible to spot half a dozen legal pads that have been used but not used up. When one of those notes is needed, it is extremely difficult to find the right pad and the right note.

High-impact time managers have broken the "scraps of paper" habit. They write all their notes to themselves in daily time logs. The Daily Time Log is a notebook used to keep track of a variety of things that previously ended up on those scraps of paper. When you use the Daily Time Log there are no little pieces of paper to get lost. Since all your reminders to yourself are in one place, you have to keep up with only one notebook.

Your Daily Time Log should be a running diary of your work life. If you set it up like the illustration in Figure 8-1, you can have a record of your appointments, have a convenient To Do List, and keep a diary of the events of the day. The Daily Time Log provides you with a permanent record of three important kinds of information in one place.

From Figure 8-1 you can see that the left-hand page is a diary that summarizes the events of the day. You can use this to make meeting notes, to write yourself reminders, to jot down ideas that occur during the day, and to provide a general summary of the day's activities.

The right-hand page serves as an appointment scheduler, an activity planner, and a To Do List. The appointment scheduler is separate from your pocket or purse calendar. However, everything on the pocket calendar should end up on your appointment scheduler or To Do List.

Your To Do List is probably the most important tool for controlling your use of time. If the right items find their way to your To Do List, you are miles ahead of the competition. If you actually stick to the items on your To Do List 75 percent of the time, you will accomplish more significant work than 95 percent of your colleagues. Here are some tactics for making best use of your To Do List:

Tactic 1: Use today's To Do List as the starting point for tomorrow's List.

Today's To Do List should contain a number of items that have been checked off as accomplishments. In all likelihood, it will also list some items that you didn't get around to today. Transfer these items to tomorrow's To Do List.

This is an important tactic that will increase your follow-through enormously. Too many people start a fresh To Do List every day, conveniently forgetting whatever they failed to ac-

Diary	Appointments	To Do
_____	8:00 _____	1.
_____	8:30 _____	2.
_____	9:00 _____	3.
_____	9:30 _____	4.
_____	10:00 _____	5.
_____	10:30 _____	6.
_____	11:00 _____	7.
_____	11:30 _____	8.
_____	12:00 _____	9.
_____	12:30 _____	10
_____	1:00 _____	11.
_____	1:30 _____	12.
_____	2:00 _____	13.
_____	2:30 _____	14.
_____	3:00 _____	15.
_____	3:30 _____	16.
_____	4:00 _____	17.
_____	4:30	18.
_____	5:00 _____	19.
_____	5:30 _____	20.
_____	6:00 _____	21.
_____	6:30 _____	22.
_____		
_____		
_____		
_____		
_____		

Figure 8-1 Daily Time Log

complish on yesterday's list. If something doesn't get done, they simply let themselves off the hook.

Transferring undone tasks to tomorrow's list makes you reexamine your priorities. Are the old items brought forward more or less important than they were yesterday? Do they still belong on the list? Has their degree of importance or urgency changed? Answering these questions forces you to keep your long-range perspective.

Tactic 2: Construct your To Do List from your calendar and your tickler file.

When you get ready to construct the day's To Do List, check your tickler file and your calendar. The tickler file will contain items that need immediate attention. Your calendar will list meetings, appointments, and deadlines for that day. Transfer these to your appointment schedule and your To Do List. Rank the items on your To Do List in order of importance.

Tactic 3: Monitor the amount of time put into each item on your To Do List compared to its importance.

Rank order the items on your To Do List with "1" being the most important. At the end of the day, write down how much time you devoted to each item. Compare the amount of time to the relative importance of each item. This comparison is particularly important for tasks that did not get completed. Did you have any high-ranking tasks that were uncompleted? How much time did you devote to these tasks? Pay particular attention to devoting more time to them tomorrow.

SUMMARY

Being organized adds power and confidence to your actions. Surprisingly, the most important tools for getting organized are relatively simple and commonplace. They consist of a desk, a calendar, a set of files, and a Daily Time Log. The effective and persisent use of these four tools can turn you into an organized and effective time manager. In short, a high-impact time manager.

CHAPTER 9

Delegation: A Key Management Skill

Delegation is one of the most effective ways to increase productivity. However, few people are really skilled at delegation. They do not know when it is appropriate to delegate, or how to make the assignment, or how to follow up on an assignment.

As a consequence, many managers overwork themselves while their subordinates frequently have little if anything to do with their time. This drives a wedge between managers and their subordinates. In such situations, managers conclude that "I work very hard, but *they* hardly work." Subordinates conclude "I'm not trusted with anything important." This means that the whole team suffers. Because they have not been given meaningful assignments, the subordinates are using low-level skills and may not have enough work to fill the day. The boss, on the other hand, spends his or her time doing tasks that are less complex and less important than those he or she should be addressing. Such a situation causes underutilization of everyone in the department.

Some of the reasons people fail to delegate effectively are the following:

1. The person who should be delegating thinks he or she can do the job easier himself or herself.
2. The delegator has been disappointed by the results produced in the past and is afraid to delegate again.
3. The delegator is afraid of losing status and power if tasks are delegated.
4. The delegator is afraid of losing control of the task and its accomplishment.
5. The delegator thinks that subordinates are not skilled enough to pull off the delegation.
6. The delegator thinks the subordinate is too lazy to do a decent job.
7. The delegator does a poor job of follow-up.

8. The delegator does a poor job of making the assignment in the beginning.
9. The delegator doesn't take the time to train subordinates to do the job.
10. The delegator feels guilty about burdening others with a task he or she can do himself or herself.
11. The delegator finds it difficult to determine who should receive which delegations.

It should be obvious that there are a large number of reasons why delegation does not work as well as it should. Yet the power of delegation to get more accomplished while developing the skill and confidence of those involved makes it worthwhile to learn the skills needed to be an effective delegator.

REASONS TO DELEGATE

Delegation usually takes place in accordance with the chain of command. The president or the chief executive officer of the organization is ultimately responsible for seeing that the mission of the organization is achieved. The CEO cannot carry out the mission single-handedly. The tasks that must be completed to achieve the mission must be divided among the small number of people reporting directly to the CEO. In turn, the tasks are divided again and again. Organizational charts and job descriptions are the formal results of this process.

However, organizational charts and job descriptions are too broad and general to ensure that everything that needs to be done actually gets done in a timely manner. That's where delegation comes in. Delegation is simply the assignment of very specific accountabilities that are tied clearly to deadlines. Generally, the things delegated are implicit within the job description. The delegation makes the responsibility and the accountability explicit.

HOW TO MAKE AN ASSIGNMENT

One of the most interesting delegation of activities used to occur at the beginning of each show of the old "Mission Impossible" television series. Peter Graves would go to some mundane yet obscure place to listen to a tape-recorded message outlining a secret mission with almost no chance of success. Graves received the ominous warning that the "Secretary will disavow any knowledge" of him or his mission if anything were to go awry. And, of course, the message would always self-destruct.

Hey, that's no way to delegate an assignment. What if Peter Graves were distracted at just the wrong moment? Self-destructing messages make it pretty tough to be sure you got the assignment right to begin with. And what kind of boss "disavows any knowledge" of you or your project when the going gets tough? However, many subordinates feel that they regularly receive "Mission Impossible" delegations.

An effective delegator makes clear assignments, sets limits, provides resources, follows up, evaluates results, and provides feedback. Most delegators are guilty of making vague assignments. The boss's mental picture of the desired results may be crystal clear, but the subordinate's picture is probably quite foggy.

Chances are that the boss spent too little time making the assignment and failed to provide enough detail for the subordinate to know exactly what is expected. These assignments tend to be verbal, are often made in an off-handed manner, and frequently have vague phrases in them like "you know what I mean" or "you get the idea, don't you." Examples of vague assignments would include

- "Handle that mess with the Whittington project."
- "See what those guys want and get rid of them."
- "Hire some good people for the data processing department."
- "Get some quotes from some other companies to see if our insurance agent is giving us a good deal."
- "Check up on how we are doing with customer complaints."

Let's look at the first one. What does handling the "mess with the Whittington project" really mean? Have you been authorized to fire the people who messed up? Should you spend thousands of dollars to appease Whittington? Can you hire subcontractors to get the project back on schedule? Are you expected to renegotiate our contract with Mr. Whittington? Are you expected to redo work that was initially approved by Whittington's representative? Are you supposed to turn Whittington into a satisfied customer or just keep him out of court? Does the mess need to be resolved today? Next week? Next month? None of these questions can be answered from looking at the assignment as it was made. The assignment was simply too vague.

Here's how the assignment should have been made. The boss should have said, "Jackson, I need to talk to you about the Whittington mess. Whittington is hot under the collar because he says we installed the wrong kind of windows for that addition to his showroom. I've made a list of what we need to do to get this thing under control."

The boss handed Jackson a piece of paper with the following items listed on it.

1. Find the blueprint and the materials specification list to see what kind of windows were actually in the contract.

2. Go out to Whittington's showroom and look at the windows. Talk to Whittington and see why he doesn't like them.

3. If it's our mistake, figure out how much it would cost us to take those windows out and get new ones installed.

4. Find out if Whittington would rather have a cash settlement rather than the windows replaced.

5. Do not spend more than $1,000 to resolve this problem.

6. Have the problem resolved by Friday at 1:00 P.M. when we have our regular staff meeting.

After he handed Jackson the paper, he sat quietly and watched Jackson's face as he read the list. When Jackson looked up, the boss asked, "Do you think that's a good approach and do you think you can pull it off by Friday?"

"If we don't have to actually pull the windows out, we can." answered Jackson.

"What if we do?"

"If I can take Dan and Keith off the Hanes project, we can have it done by next Wednesday. Will that do?"

"Sure. Any other questions?" asked the boss.

"Yeah, one more. If he'd settle for money instead of new windows, what's the most I can offer?" asked Jackson.

"Start with $500. In no case go above the $1,000 limit," the boss responded.

"Fine. I'll keep you posted," answered Jackson.

Nodding to Jackson, the boss said, "Good. If you need anything on this, let me know."

As Jackson left the office, the boss made a note in his calendar to follow up with Jackson this coming Thursday morning.

Notice the difference between these two assignments. The first was a brief, vague, one-way communication. The second assignment was different. It was specific and detailed. The boss was quite clear about what constituted "the mess" and about the results expected. The boss made it clear how much money and how many people would be available to fix the mess. The boss encouraged Jackson to ask questions and to share pertinent information. Most important of all, the boss set a deadline.

One of the big differences between the two approaches to this particular delegation is the assumptions made by the boss and the subordinate. In the first instance, the boss made too many incorrect assumptions. He assumed that making the assignment would be quick, simple, and easy. Then he assumed that the subordinate shared his or her understanding of the nature and importance of the task assigned. Finally he assumed that the subordinate understood the assignment.

This set of assumptions usually leads to disappointment. The boss is mystified by the length of time it takes to do exactly the wrong thing. The subordinate is disappointed because the boss seems unappreciative of the results produced and the effort expended. Yet these two will continue to disappoint each other unless they learn to communicate more accurately.

Both are at fault. The boss is at fault for failure to be clear in making the delegation. The subordinate is at fault for taking on an assignment without insisting on a full understanding of the expectations.

Vague delegation doesn't have to prevail. Six steps can make all the difference:

1. Develop a clear picture of the results that are to be achieved by the person receiving the delegation.

2. Encourage the person receiving the delegation to ask questions and to share information about the situation.

3. Provide sufficient resources to get the job done. Be very clear with your subordinate about what resources are available.

4. Set a deadline that is realistic but challenging.

5. Put the assignment in writing, making everything as specific and concrete as possible.

6. Follow up on the assignment. And do not wait until the last minute to follow-up. Follow-up early enough to allow sufficient time to fix any problems discovered.

From the subordinate's side there are also a set of rules for handling a delegated assignment. When receiving an assignment, the subordinate should

1. Ask enough questions to make certain the assignment is understood.

2. Find out if you have a budget or can expect help from other people in the organization.

3. Work with your boss to set a deadline that is mutually satisfactory.

4. Give your boss regular feedback about how the assignment is going.

SUMMARY

Delegation is one of the most powerful tools available to a person. When you work in any group, projects have to be subdivided into jobs, and jobs have to be subdivided into tasks. While one person may have responsibility for a large project, it is unlikely that one person will be able to do all the tasks that are required to complete the projects. Certain jobs and tasks will have to be delegated. Effective managers delegate in a complete and detailed manner. They also follow up on the delegation to make certain that the project is on track.

CHAPTER 10

Controlling
Time
and
Accomplishments:
The
Managed
Day

ONE DAY AT A TIME

Time is fixed. Time is available to us in standard and unvarying units. We need reminding of this fact because we experience time subjectively. When we are waiting for the tax return check, time seems to drag. Vacations seem to fly by. Regardless of our perceptions, however, every day is really composed of 24 hours, each of which is exactly 60 minutes long.

Accomplishments, on the other hand, are variable. Consider two employees. Alana Wilson, an audit supervisor for a Big Eight accounting firm, packs more accomplishments into a day than any other supervisor in her office. Another supervisor in the same office, Jack Loren, gets little, if anything, done. Both had the same amount of time. What was the difference between these two people?

The difference was *how* each hour was used. Alana used the hours of the day to produce a predetermined set of results. Jack drifted through the day responding to whatever and to whomever came along. Consequently, Jack had little to show for the time spent. The difference is not accidental. Alana's accomplishments were the results of a set of attitudes and skills that led to effective time management.

Sustained accomplishment requires that the attitudes and skills of high-impact time management be brought to bear on the work of each day. The high-impact time manager knows that the time management contest is won or lost based on the way each small block of time is handled. The high-impact time manager strives to have a "managed day."

The managed day is one that is controlled. The activities of the day are planned for the most part. The unplanned activities focus primarily on meeting important objectives of the organization or the individual. The high-impact time manager knows what results he or she wishes to produce for the day. Every effort is made to see that time is used to produce those results. When interruptions or crises occur, the high-impact time manager minimizes the amount of time spent on them and gets back to tasks that will contribute to meeting the goals planned for the day.

The high-impact time manager worries about small blocks of time for a very good reason. We can examine the way we used time in the past, we can plan the way we will use time in the future, but we can *control* only the time we use right now. Failure to exercise proper control means that the time is wasted or lost. Seizing control of the present shapes the future. Controlling the present is the only way of transforming dreams for the future into reality.

Another reason for focusing on small blocks of time is our limited attention spans. The mind is restless, constantly scanning the environment for novelty, ruminating on the past, and speculating about the future. Our limited attention spans cause many of our time management problems. A limited attention span is the culprit when the mind strays in midsentence while talking to a customer. Similarly, a limited attention span causes us to forget what we were doing before the most recent interruption. It is also the reason we sometimes welcome the opportunity to socialize when we should be paying attention to our work.

HAVE A PLAN FOR THE DAY

Most people extol the virtues of planning, but far fewer structure their day with a plan. It is easier to endorse the idea of planning than it is to muster the self-discipline to create daily plans and, more important, to implement them. However, starting the day without a plan almost guarantees that you will waste a significant amount of time and accomplish far less than would have been possible.

People resist planning for a variety of reasons. Most of the reasons sound plausible, but close examination reveals that they are rationalizations. Check out the following rationalizations for not planning and see how many apply to you.

Rationalization 1: I have so many urgent tasks to deal with that I can't plan.

Responsibilities mount, tasks pile upon tasks, and each request is more urgent than the last. Most people, managers in particular, experience a sense of urgency about their life. There never seems to be enough time to get everything done. We find ourselves hurrying from one thing to the next.

The urge to hurry makes it almost impossible to pay more than fleeting attention to things that are not urgent. Even important things receive little attention if they are not urgent. However, failure to plan simply creates more crises that demand urgent attention.

Rationalization 2: I'm too busy to plan.

The days are already full. Perhaps not everything is urgent, but there are more than enough routine tasks to keep you busy. An unending round of meetings is followed by a flood of requests. The ringing telephone and other interruptions punctuate the day. The good intentions that launched the day are swept away by the rush of events. There is too little time to plan, and unanticipated demands would simply sidetrack whatever plans were made. This rationalization sounds good until the results of a typical busy but unplanned day are examined. At the end of such a day, generally little of importance has been accomplished. In fact, most people are hard pressed to remember what kept them so busy throughout the day.

Rationalization 3: It is futile to plan since the future is unpredictable.

Plans attempt to shape and structure the future. However, many people regard the future as largely unpredictable. From this perspective, plans are virtually useless because we inevitably guess wrong about how the future is going to look. The best approach, according to this rationalization, is to hang loose and be prepared to be flexible. However, this view is too passive and pessimistic. While the future is uncertain, the broad shape of events is frequently apparent. Under these circumstances, plans are prudent.

For example, it is quite clear that the number of people over the age of 65 will increase dramatically in the next 15 to 20 years. It is clear that the market for baby booties will stagnate while the market for retirement annuities is going to soar. Prudent firms will devise products and marketing plans to tap this segment of the market.

Rationalization 4: Planning limits your options.

A plan specifies what you will do and, by implication, what you will not do. This makes planning a rather risky business for the person who is apprehensive about being judged by results. A plan spells out the results you hope to accomplish. This puts you on the spot. If the plan is not accomplished, you have to explain what went wrong. Without a plan, no explanations are necessary. It is more comfortable to coast along without addressing the pressure a plan represents.

When you overcome the rationalizations, you are ready to begin serious planning. On the one hand, planning a day is a relatively straightforward task. You list everything that needs to be done that day and arrange the list in sequence according to importance or required timing. Start at the beginning and keep after it until the tasks are completed. Simple, right?

On the other hand, planning a day is quite complex. You need to respond to a number of urgent tasks. You need to ignore some things that appear to be equally urgent. You need to make time for some important tasks that are not particularly urgent. There will be a number of interruptions during the day, and you will have to attend one or more pointless meetings. You realize that the day will be over before you can possibly get everything done you want to do. Devising a plan with these problems in mind is anything but simple and straightforward.

The first problem is the one of priority. The total number of tasks or problems that will or should demand your attention on a given day are quite large. Too many, in fact, for you to respond to them all. Things will be left undone. This is true even of the most effective time manager. Given that it is impossible to do everything, tasks must be assigned priorities. You must have a method for determining which things *must* be done, which things *should* be done, and which things can be safely ignored.

Establishing priorities depends on the goals you aspire to accomplish. You could determine your goals on a daily basis, but that would limit you to dealing with urgent matters only. One of the things that separates high achievers from also-rans is the way the former deals with matters that are not yet urgent. This means that the priorities that govern daily planning must be derived from long-range plans and projects.

On a practical basis, this means your daily To Do List must

be drawn up in light of weekly, monthly, quarterly, and annual goals. This is an issue covered in detail in Chapter 12, "Turning Long-Term Goals into Daily Achievements." There is only one way to make sure that your "managed day," as scheduled by your To Do List, will lead you in the direction of your long-range goals. You must start with your long-range goals and work backward.

Your planning should be fully integrated over time. Your five-year goals should fall into place automatically if you make your annual goals for the next five years. Your annual goals should fall into place if you make your quarterly goals for the year. Your quarterly goals should be a cinch if you meet each of your monthly goals. Similarly, meeting your weekly goals should lead inevitably to meeting your monthly goals. Finally, meeting your daily goals should guarantee meeting your weekly goals.

From this perspective, the To Do List assumes considerable importance. It is your key time management tool when coordinated with your long-range goals. When it is not linked to your long-range goals, it is merely a scrap of paper that may or may not contain a useful set of tasks.

Of course, our point is that the To Do List should be your keystone for managing your time. If you are unwilling to use a To Do List, you are not serious about improving your time management skills. If you are unwilling to link your long-range goals to the To Do List, you may get more done, but there is little likelihood that you will actually accomplish your major goals in life.

Your To Do List should be devised before your workday starts, preferably the day before. Many effective time managers spend the last half hour of their workday putting together the next day's list. If you are not sure which way is better for you, conduct an experiment. Try composing tomorrow's To Do List as the last task of the day for one week. Then try putting the list together the first thing in the morning for a week. After the two weeks are over, evaluate the results. Did you get more done one way or the other? Were you less likely to leave something out one way or the other? Which way was more comfortable? After answering these questions, pick the better way, stick with it for six months, and reevaluate.

People who have mastered the use of the To Do List share a surprisingly similar set of tactics. All find the list something that they use every day, not just when they feel like it. Almost all use the list in conjunction with a calendar. Most use the list for nonwork activities as well as work-related tasks. In addition to these general approaches, here are some tips that should help you master the use of the To Do List:

1. **Develop time norms for tasks you do regularly.** If you must write a client contact report on a weekly basis, time how long it takes you to get this done. Knowing this information will allow you to schedule a realistic amount of time on this job. If you drive your child to school, know how much time this requires and plug it into your schedule.

2. **Set aside large blocks of time to work on major projects.** This is perhaps the most important tip. Large blocks of time are required to make significant progress on major projects. Scheduling large blocks of time makes it possible to deal with projects that are important but not urgent. These are the first items you should place on your To Do List. Scheduling large blocks of time for large, important projects will ensure that you do not end up disappointed. This tactic is of such importance that it is discussed in detail in Chapter 12.

3. **Find time to plan by making an appointment with yourself.** This is the solution to the problem of being too busy to plan. If you have an appointment with someone else, you manage to keep it—even if you suspect the meeting will be of little importance. Well, treat yourself with as much respect. Make an appointment with yourself and *keep it.* Shut your door and don't allow yourself to be disturbed. Use this time to plan and, and important, schedule high-impact projects.

4. **Rank your tasks for the day by priority and tackle the high-priority items first.** This approach will ensure the best use of your time. If you invest your time in the highest-priority items, you are gaining maximum payoff from the time invested. You never have to worry about what you should do next because your list spells that out clearly.

5. **When you make up tomorrow's To Do List, carry forward the items you did not get to on today's list.** This procedure will guarantee that things do not slip through the cracks. If you follow this practice conscientiously, you will eliminate those things you "meant to get around to but forgot."

6. **Batch short tasks together.** Set aside a time during the day for dealing with the nagging, niggling little things. If you deal with several little items at once, none of them have an opportunity to throw you off track as an interruption. This reduces the start-stop problems that occur when you are interrupted.

7. **Whenever feasible, complete a task once you have started it.** When a task is interrupted, you have several problems associated with getting started again. Sometimes you will be distracted and never get back to the task. In this case, all the time you have already invested is wasted. At other times, you get back to the task, but you may waste a significant amount of time getting reoriented to the problem.

STAY ON TRACK

Your plan tells you how your time should be used. A good To Do List will rank your tasks and show how much time you expect to devote to each one. If you follow your plan and your To Do List, accomplishing your goals would be a cinch. However, the world is not simple enough to allow this to happen with any regularity.

There will be important things you forget to put on the list that *must* be addressed. Some people will telephone you unexpectedly, and others will stick their heads in your office door and ask you if you have a minute. Your boss will toss an unexpected problem at you that has to be handled immediately. The kids may get sick and need to be picked up from school.

SUMMARY

Time has to be managed one day at a time. We are either effective or ineffective time managers on a daily basis. Planning for the future is essential, but managing the small blocks of time we receive each day is the real work of creating the future.

We reach our long-term goals to the extent that we are able to manage our day. A carefully managed day makes it possible to link long-term goals to daily activities. The cumulative effect of staying on track on a daily basis leads to the accomplishment of major long-term goals.

CHAPTER 11

Goal Setting: The Engine of Accomplishment

THE KEYSTONE

If we could address only one subject on the topic of time management, that topic would be goal setting. Goal setting is the single most powerful tool available for managing time or achieving results. This is a strong statement, we know, but this is one time when hard-boiled practical people and scholarly researchers agree almost completely. People who set goals get more accomplished than those who do not. They also get things done more quickly.

Goal setting is also one of the more straightforward techniques available to people who want to manage time more effectively. The process of goal setting is easy to understand and easy to implement. If you are not currently a goal setter, get ready for information that will transform your approach to getting what you want from life. If you are a goal setter, we have a few new tricks for you.

THE IMPORTANCE OF SETTING GOALS

All of us have had goals from time to time. When you were a teenager you probably had a goal of getting your driver's license as soon as you were 16 years old. Since then you may have had goals about saving money for a down payment for a house or a goal of taking a vacation in some exotic location before a certain age. You may have had career goals associated with earning raises, getting promotions, or attaining certain levels of income. However, if you are like most people, you are not a systematic goal setter.

You may set a single goal when you really want something, but do you have other goals to address when you have achieved the first one? Is your goal setting sporadic and uncoordinated? If so, you are not reaping the full benefits of goal setting. You are not having the impact you could have in life. Your time is not being put to its highest and best use.

We want our lives and our efforts to matter. We want other people to

- Pay attention to us.
- Care about what we think and feel.
- Listen to what we have to say.
- Respond to our needs and desires.

We want our lives to have an impact on the world around us. The more ambitious we are, the greater our desire to make our impact felt.

Many of us judge our effectiveness as human beings by how much impact we have. Winners find a way to have an impact regardless of their endeavor or location in the world. For some, that impact may be measured in terms of building a business or inventing a better way to grow food. For others it may be writing a beautiful symphony or rearing a productive, emotionally healthy child. People have impact when they are able to adapt to a new situation and influence events in that situation.

Winners always seem to rise above the turmoil and make things happen. They seem to get things done, to get others to do things effectively, and to make others glad they are part of the team. Frequently, they are able to produce these results without investing more time than people who get very little accomplished. The winners have greater impact because they focus their energy on goals. Not only do they have goals, but they have goals that are important for their careers, their organizations, and their personal lives.

Goals provide you with a way to direct and structure your time. If you have no goals, it is simply impossible to waste time. Goals provide the standards against which you measure your activities. If an activity contributes to meeting a high-priority goal, it is an effective use of time. If an activity is unrelated to accomplishing a goal, it is a waste of time.

Goals provide parameters and measuring sticks for judging the effective use of time. Goals provide identifiable and measurable milestones for evaluating progress. Without goals, the concept of the effective use of time has little meaning. Without goals, the concept of the *efficient* use of time is completely meaningless.

Not all goals are created equal. Some goals are motivational; some are not. Some goals are beneficial to the organization and the individual; some are not. Some goals clarify what is expected; some confuse. This chapter will show you how to set goals that will motivate you to achieve more at work and have a more fulfilling life outside your work.

GETTING READY TO SET GOALS

Goal setting works because it focuses attention and effort. Most people achieve relatively little because their efforts and resources are dissipated by a multitude of activities. Even people who have goals may fall far short of their potential if they cannot bring energy and force to their efforts.

Busyness is not accomplishment. A flurry of activity does not necessarily produce results. The illusion of accomplishment created by busyness is called the "activity trap." Being busy and having responsibilities are not enough. Constantly hurrying will not necessarily increase your impact on the world around you. Impact is created when the *right goals* are attacked with vigor and conviction.

Enthusiasm for achieving a goal is essential. As Ralph Waldo Emerson put it, "Nothing great was ever accomplished without enthusiasm." Others have used phrases such as "burning desire" and "fire in the belly" to describe the enthusiasm needed to accomplish ambitious goals.

It is one thing to recommend enthusiasm. It is quite another to develop it when you do not already have a "keen interest" or feel "fervor." The techniques of time management, including goal setting, will seem to be mechanical and bothersome without enthusiasm. Unless you develop enthusiasm, you will soon conclude that time management is more trouble than it is worth.

Enthusiasm is generated by a vision or dream important enough to make you confront and overcome the obstacles that must be faced every day. A vision or dream inspires when it is personally meaningful. For some, the vision is a series of promotions leading to the president's suite of a major corporation. Others dream of starting their own businesses. For still others, the vision might be a college education for their children. Some people dream of doing something about the lack of adequate medical care for the poor or simply providing financial security for their own retirement. The vision or dream gets its power by tapping deep needs or aspirations of the individual.

The high-impact time manager links goals to these visions or dreams. When goals are tied to powerful and stimulating visions or dreams, enthusiasm is generated. The following steps help harness the power of visions to the accomplishment of goals.

1. **Elaborate and specify your dream or vision in detail.**

   This process, called visualization, adds reality and strength to the dream. If your vision is to provide for your retirement security, visualize your retirement in great detail. Form a mental picture of where you will live, how you will look, how you will feel, and what you will do.

   Picture yourself looking at the free-and-clear deed of your home. Visualize the bank book with an adequate cash reserve. Visualize the annuity check and other retirement income you would need to make your retirement secure. Picture yourself feeling comfortable about having enough financial security to travel wherever you want to go and do whatever you want to do. Don't you feel yourself developing the enthusiasm it takes to strive for financial security?

2. **Develop long-range that would lead to the accomplishment of your vision.**

   The high-impact time manager budgets time to deal with tasks according to their priorities and potential impact. This was called *macro time management* in Chapter 2. A task's priority comes from the contribution it makes to accomplishing your dream or making your vision a reality. However, the link between daily tasks or lifelong dreams is frequently unclear. Long-range plans clarify that link.

3. **Break down your long-range plans into short-term goals.**

   Plans for long-term goals are inevitably complex. However, they can almost always be subdivided into small, less complicated steps. These smaller steps are your goals. Depending on your vision and your plan, some of the goals will be daily goals, and others will be weekly, monthly, or quarterly goals. In any case, the goals and their associated priorities provide direction and focus for your daily activities.

4. **Transform your short-term goals into activities for your daily To Do List.**
    Time can only be managed in small blocks. You control the actual use of your time on a moment-to-moment basis. Unless those goals that lead to your long-range plans and vision are part of *today's* To Do List, you are off track. Plans are useless unless they are implemented, and they can *only* be implemented in the fleeting present.

High-impact time managment works because it makes a secure link between the long term (vision) and the short term (the To Do List). Macro time management transforms the ephemeral vision or dream into concrete tasks that must be accomplished today. The future is shaped and our visions are realized by careful attention to controlling the present.

In addition to enthusiasm, self-confidence and conviction are required. Ambitious goals are accomplished by those who believe they can. Belief in their own abilities or effort gives achievers the power and the persistence to overcome whatever obstacles stand between them and their goals.

A GOAL-SETTING SYSTEM THAT WORKS

Goal setting has the potential for increasing motivation and influencing the way time and other resources are used. However, all goals are not created equally. Goals that are vague and unrealistic are not taken seriously. Goals that do not make a contribution to the realization of a dream or a vision will not motivate or inspire. Goals that produce results have the following characteristics:

Goal-Setting Principle 1: A goal should be specific.

Goals that are specific and detailed produce better results than do goals that are general. Setting a quota of ten prospecting telephone calls a day produces better results than does the instruction to "do your best." Specific goals reduce confusion and clarify what is expected.

Taking aim at a target, an archer looks only at the bull's-eye. All extraneous stimuli are ignored. A specific goal acts as bull's-eye. The instruction to "do your best" often results in people painting the target around the arrow, regardless of where it landed.

Goal-Setting Principle 2: A goal should be measured.

Goals are far more likely to be achieved if they are measurable. A goal of "promoting student development" is not likely to have much impact on the behavior of either teachers or students. As stated, the goal is not measurable. How would anyone know when it has been accomplished?

Here is a measurable goal related to student development: "Increase the reading comprehension of fourth grade students during the next academic year by 1.5 years as measured by the California Achievement Test." Stated this way, the goal is far more likely to change behavior and get results. We can tell whether or not the goal has been achieved. Even if the goal is not met, we will at least have an accurate measure of the amount of progress made.

Notice that the measurable goal statement has three components. First, it identified the people involved (fourth grade students). Second, it specified quantitatively the exact results to be achieved (1.5 year improvement in reading comprehension scores). Third, it specified a deadline or time frame. These three components are required for the goal to be measurable. If the goal is not measurable, it is merely a platitude or a good intention.

Goal-Setting Principle 3: A goal should be challenging.

Challenging goals are motivational. If you want someone to expend effort on a goal, the task should be neither too easy nor too difficult. If the goal is too easy, people lose interest quickly. Few people are interested in "shooting fish in a barrel." Chess is a more interesting game than is checkers because it is more challenging. If a goal is too difficult, people tend to give up quickly, assuming that the task is "impossible." The trick is to set the goal high enough to cause the person to "stretch" but low enough to attain.

A challenging goal is not some pie-in-the-sky pipedream. Sales trainers know that a salesperson who has been selling $200,000 a year cannot use goal setting or any other technique to increase his or her sales to $2,000,000 instantly. This is foolish fantasy—not goal setting. If a goal is much more than one-third higher than previous levels of accomplishment, it simply will not be taken seriously. When setting the difficulty of a goal, it is generally useful to involve the person who will have to achieve the results. After all, that person's belief that the goal is realistic is a key factor in its accomplishment.

Goal-Setting Principle 4: Make the goal a present reality.

Setting goals is looking into the future. However, action is possible only in the present. This paradox turns much of goal setting into an exercise in good intentions and repeated disappointment. For goal setting to work, present actions must be linked to plans for the future.

To have real meaning, goals must be broken down into three categories:

- Long-range goals cover several years, but probably not more than ten.
- Intermediate goals are set by breaking down long-range goals into annual or quarterly sets of goals that lead toward the long-range goals.
- Short-range goals come from breaking down your intermediate goals into monthly or weekly steps toward your long-range goals.

When goals are set using this procedure, everything you do tomorrow will have a definite impact on where you will be five years from now. It is a way of making your long-range goals a present reality of your daily life. When your daily tasks are tied to long-range goals, you can easily distinguish between work that produces results and just staying busy.

Goal-Setting Principle 5: Set deadlines for goals.

Goals without deadlines are merely good intentions. Deadlines are the way you put teeth into your goals—the way you make them hold you like a vise.

Most people do not accomplish their goals because their timetables are vague and can easily slip. Real results are produced when specific goals are given definite deadlines. An amazing number of things can be accomplished when you exercise the self-discipline needed to meet serious deadlines.

Goal-Setting Principle 6: Set goals that inspire your commitment.

Self-discipline is difficult. Setting goals is not enough; you must be able to stick to the goals you set. Some people can sit down and come up with goals that will make them rich and famous in short order, but nothing ever really seems to happen.

The most frequent problem is that their goals provide no inspiration, the imagination is not stimulated. The desire that stimulates action and makes self-discipline possible is missing. The stronger the desire for a certain goal, the easier it is to generate the required self-discipline.

For example, few people would be inspired to increase their productivity by 15 percent next year simply to prove to themselves they could do it. But if the reward for a 15 percent increase in productivity were a new sports car—if the sports car is greatly prized—the necessary self-discipline would probably be forthcoming. If you want to make goal setting really work, choose only goals that captivate your whole mind and all your emotions. Set your sights on something you can really get excited about, and self-discipline will be easy.

Goal-Setting Principle 7: Treat your goals as serious promises.

Most of us try hard to keep the promises we make. We are willing to come in early, stay late, or work weekends to keep a promise you made to the boss. If we promise the kids that they could go to a certain movie, we make every effort to ensure that it happens. However, most of us are not nearly so good at keeping promises to ourselves. Maybe that is why other people always seem to have more confidence in us than we have in ourselves.

What causes people to be more unreliable to themselves than to others? One reason may be that others tend to hold us to our promises, while we tend to be easier on ourselves. This is especially true if we are overcommitted to other people. Goals really work when we consider them to be promises we make to ourselves that are just as important as promises we make to other people. We need to keep them with the same tenacity with which we keep a promise made to anyone else.

If you have a particular problem keeping promises to yourself, try this exercise. Write down your promises to yourself. Write them in the form of a legal contract, complete with rewards for meeting the contract and penalties for failure to perform. While this may be a little extreme, it makes a point. You should treat your goals seriously.

SETTING GOALS WITH OTHER PEOPLE

There are times when you are involved in helping others set goals. It may be people who work for you, family members, or folks at the local PTA. Establishing goals for other people or with other people is tricky business. While the goals need to be specific, measurable, and challenging, they also need to generate commitment.

To generate commitment, the goals must relate to important values or needs of the people who have to accomplish them. If you assign goals or set quotas, there is a good chance that they will not tap the values or needs required for motivation. If you simply impose goals, as you may be tempted to do with your subordinates or family members, the goals are likely to have little inspirational power. Worse, imposed goals can cause subtle resistance or open rebellion.

A better approach is to establish mutually agreed-upon goals. When goals are mutually agreed upon, the possibility of conflict and resentment are reduced. The following principles will help you when you set goals with others:

Mutual Goal-Setting Principle 1: Review priorities to make certain that everyone involved agrees on what is important to the goal-setting task.

Goals obtain their motivational force from their link to important values and cherished dreams. Goals have the power to inspire action when they are aligned with important priorities. If you begin your goal setting with a review of what is really important in the long run, the goals have a greater likelihood of being linked with things that are important to the person who will tackle the goal.

This review of priorities does not have to involve a lengthy, abstract, philosophical dissertation on the nature of ultimate values. If the task before the PTA committee is the planning of a Halloween carnival, it is not necessary to discuss the theory of humor in preadolescents or microeconomic theory. However, it will probably be helpful to remind the committee that we want the kids to have fun and the PTA to raise some money. Such a reminder will keep your committee from wasting time on tangents, and will add importance to the accomplishment of apparently trivial goals.

Mutual Goal-Setting Principle 2: Involve the people who have to accomplish the goal in setting the goal.

Participation in goal setting leads to greater commitment in achieving the goals. When people participate in setting objectives, they are likely to regard them as meaningful. Participation ensures that everyone understands the importance of the goals to the organization. When people participate, they will negotiate for goals that allow them to serve their own needs while meeting organizational demands.

Goals set by mutual agreement are more likely to be realistic. The closer we get to the people in the trenches, the more likely the goals are to be realistic. These people understand the specifics of a situation far better than anyone from the home office possibly could. Obstacles that may be invisible in the home office loom large on the front lines.

Mutual Goal-Setting Principle 3: Review with everyone involved how the goals they are setting must be coordinated with other goals.

The completion of large projects requires that the goals of many different individuals be coordinated. A wedding reception is a complex event involving a large number of people with different responsibilities. The florist and the caterer each have a separate set of goals to accomplish that must meet demanding standards. However, their goals must be coordinated with each other to produce the desired result.

Time must be invested in coordinating the goals of people working on the same project. Similarly, if one person's work is an input for someone else's work, careful coordination is required. Recently, great improvements have been made in inventory control by more closely coordinating the shipment of raw materials from suppliers.

This new approach, called just-in-time inventory, requires suppliers to make many more smaller shipments to the customer. While typical inventory systems stockpile enough raw materials to last weeks or months, the just-in-time system frequently allows a company to unload raw materials just hours before it is needed in the manufacturing process. Just-in-time systems can save large companies literally millions of dollars a year in inventory carrying costs. Such is the power of coordinating the goals of people who work together.

Mutual Goal-Setting Principle 4: Provide sufficient resources to accomplish the goal.

This characteristic is rather obvious, but many people overlook it. High goals, properly set, will result in higher output. However, this greater output is not without cost. In a sales setting, explicit goals calling for more sales calls will also require more travel, the use of more sales materials, more postage, more telephone expenses, and greater entertainment expenditures. Unless resources are made available to support the accomplishment of the goals set, the full benefits of goal setting will not be realized.

If the necessary resources to accomplish the goals are not made available, goal setting can backfire. Motivation can decrease instead of increase. If output expectations change without a corresponding increase in inputs, many people conclude that the top management is not really serious about meeting the goals. An even more damaging interpretation of the situation is possible. If additional resources are not forthcoming, some employees may suspect that the organization expects to take the additional productivity "out of our hides."

> Mutual Goal-Setting Principle 5: Provide rewards for the accomplishment of goals.

The satisfaction of completing a goal is a powerful motivator in and of itself. Much greater motivation and satisfaction occur when rewards are tied to the accomplishment of goals. While monetary goals are appropriate for many situations, praise and recognition always should be used as rewards when goals are met.

Organizations that have worked hardest at linking rewards to performance generally outperform other firms in the industry. Lincoln Electric Company, manufacturer of arc welding equipment, has the lowest labor costs and the highest quality in its industry. Lincoln Electric workers are paid bonuses based on overall output and for suggestions that improve the operation of the organization. At Nucor Steel, one of the few bright spots in the U.S. steel industry, workers are paid annual bonuses based on meeting performance goals. These bonuses average about 50 percent of the workers' base pay. Both Lincoln Electric and Nucor are profit leaders in their industries.

GOALS FOR LIFE AFTER WORK

Goal setting as described can make a tremendous difference in your accomplishments at work. But goal setting can be applied with equal success to other parts of your life. When you set goals for your career, you will find that you will get more done in less time. What you do with the extra time will make a big difference in the quality of your life.

Some of the time liberated by goal setting should be invested in your career. The extra time devoted to career concerns will pay handsome dividends in terms of new skills learned and positioning yourself for advancement. However, much of the additional time made available by effective goal setting should be invested in leisure and personal relationships. While striving for both efficiency and effectiveness in your career, you should avoid making it the sole or even primary source of your satisfactions.

When work crowds out every other aspect of life, you have become a workaholic. A workaholic approach to your career is detrimental to both you and the organization in the long run. Leisure (as contrasted to idleness) is valuable for two reasons. First, leisure allows you to pursue interests that you value highly for their own sakes. Second, properly pursued leisure relaxes, refreshes, and restores. Leisure allows you to recharge your batteries for the competitive fray of your career. From this perspective, leisure and recreation become necessities.

The balanced life-style includes personal relationships. The most important investment you can make in a relationship is time. And the time invested in a relationship should not be polluted by career concerns. The time devoted to a relationship should include a significant amount of undivided attention, which is essential for the growth and nurturing of a relationship.

In addition to providing you with more personal time, goal setting can also enrich your nonwork time. Many people fail to reap the full benefits of setting goals because they confine the process to their careers. High achievers can fail miserably with their personal lives. They may use goal setting to tackle great challenges at work, but they never seem to understand the benefits of applying the same principles to their family lives.

A balanced life-style generally requires goal setting in a wide range of areas: career, financial, family, recreation, social, personal, and physical fitness. Goals should be set for every area of your life that is important to you.

Here is a mental experiment to help you decide whether or not you have a planned set of goals. Imagine that you found out that you had only six months to live. Then list the things you would do with those six months. You will probably be surprised at the things you would cram into those few months. If your list contains a number of things you are not currently planning to do, your goal set is probably unbalanced in favor of your career. After you have thought about these issues, why not set some goals that will get you busy doing some of these neglected things right away.

EXPANDING HORIZONS

One of the greatest benefits of setting goals and living by them is that they keep bringing you to a place where you can set bigger and better goals. An accomplished goal is a stepping stone to greater goals. Using goals as stepping stones enables you to keep expanding your horizons.

Earlier in the chapter we argued that goals derive their power from dreams or vision. That power is neither mystical nor magical. Very solid psychological research has shown that the techniques of visualization and covert rehearsal can significantly improve performance of various tasks. Evoking desirable dreams or visions provides more meaning for the incremental goals that will lead to the realization of those dreams and visions.

Your dreams provide the fuel that keeps you going when you encounter obstacles in the path to your goal. Practical people of great accomplishment have an abundance of ambitious dreams. Their practicality is reflected in their goal setting. They believe in their dreams enough to develop a set of goals that will inevitably lead to the accomplishment of their dreams. Then they patiently set about accomplishing those goals in the proper sequence.

Obviously, practical dreamers do not always accomplish their dreams. They know defeat and discouragement. Some of their dreams are never realized. Some are realized only after long delay and tribulation. And sometimes a greater dream is realized along the way almost by accident.

Christopher Columbus never succeeded in sailing West to China and India. He accomplished a greater, but unexpected, dream of discovering the New World. Yet it would be a mistake to assume that Columbus discovered the Americas by accident. It was no accident that he was sailing toward an ambitious goal. Without the dream of finding a new route to the East, Columbus would have continued to lead an uneventful life following established sea routes.

Albert Einstein failed to achieve his goal of developing a unified field theory explaining the relationshiop between the major forces in the universe. However, he was an astounding achiever, unafraid to strive for incredibly ambitious dreams. Our greatest achievers eagerly dream on the cosmic scale.

The practical lesson for those of us who lack Columbus's spirit of adventure and Einstein's genius is that dreams are the seed of reality. Since dreams are so important to achievement, we should quit suppressing them and begin to welcome them as allies to be strengthened and developed.

CHAPTER 12

Turning Long-Term Goals Into Daily Achievements

Stories of high-achieving people inspire and motivate. The stories sometimes take on the proportions of myths and legends. The best loved of these stories have two common elements. First, the person who is the focus of the story must have a challenging and worthy vision or dream. Second, the person must encounter and overcome obstacles to make the dream a reality. Typically, we respond to the characteristics of creativity, persistence, and courage displayed by high achievers. In short, we see and are inspired by the heroics in such stories.

We seldom see that there is another side to the accomplishments of the world's great achievers. This is the more mundane side of high achievement, consisting of planning, scheduling, coordinating, and following up on tasks large and small. This side of achievement is fairly boring—but essential. The magic is often in the details.

The most inspiring goals in the world have to be transplanted into what has to be done between now and the end of the workday. Planning and scheduling translate long-term goals into manageable daily tasks that belong on a To Do list. The discipline involved in following up on activities that have to be coordinated keeps projects on time. Not heroic, but essential.

As we shall see, the principles of planning are basically the same regardless of the activity or its scope. Nervous mothers feverishly planning their daughters' weddings use most of the techniques employed by Eisenhower in mapping the Allies' strategy for the invasion of Europe.

Everyone plans. You plan the vacations you take, the movies you want to see, and the route you drive to work. Planning may be as simple as driving to the corner store for a quart of milk or as complex as coordinating a $50 million worldwide advertising campaign involving activities on five continents. But there are vast differences between sporadic planning and doing it consistently and persistently with as little struggle and effort as possible. Driving to the convenience store requires far less planning than conducting marketing research, buying advertising time, and handling the other details of a massive marketing program.

WELL-LAID PLANS

Did Pete Rose break Ty Cobb's all-time base hit record by swinging at every pitch throughout his baseball career? Did Joe Girard earn the title of the World's Greatest Salesman through sheer luck? Did Sir Edmund Hillary climb Mount Everest on impulse? Of course not. This trio of achievers reached the pinnacles of their professions by achieving powerfully motivating goals through careful planning and skillful execution. Planning was their vehicle to success. Planning multiplied their power and shaped their actions. Each began to lay the necessary groundwork years before the results were achieved.

True, Rose, Girard, and Hillary had their share of the "breaks," but those breaks were often opportunities they created for themselves. Their breaks were the results of planning, preparation, and organization. Planning adds a powerful dimension of control. While planning obviously improves the control you have over routine task, planning also makes it possible to get better control of "breaks," "accidents," and "opportunities." According to time management consultant Alan Lakein, planning brings the future into the present. By planning, you can do something with the future right now.

This kind of planning focuses on actions that implement our objectives. Without goals and objectives, planning is useless. The relationship between setting objectives and developing plans is as close as you can get. Effective planning translates objectives into reality through a systematic series of tasks and activities. Planning is the road map for accomplishment. Good planning provides you with landmarks and milestones that point the way and allow you to gauge your progress.

THE PARADOX OF PLANNING

Despite the obvious importance of planning, it is something most people dread. Most people plan haphazardly and do so only with great reluctance. While recognizing the importance of planning, many people have numerous plausible excuses to avoid planning:

1. I don't have time to plan.
2. I want to keep my options open.
3. I'm not good at planning.
4. Why should I? Things are going fine without planning.
5. We are just a little outfit and planning is for the big guys.

However appealing these excuses may be, they undermine your effectiveness. If you fail to plan, you will not necessarily be a failure. However, you will achieve more of your potential if you become a planner. Planning clarifies expectations and directs actions toward desired goals. Far too often, people look back on life and realize how many more things could have been accomplished if they had set goals and planned their work to meet their goals.

People who are skillful planners have greater control of their destinies than do those who "go with the flow." While some spontaneous pleasures come from going with the flow, it also subjects you to some nasty surprises. Planning will not prevent interruptions, emergencies, or unanticipated crises. Planning should reduce these to the minimum, however. A plan also helps you get back on track quickly when you have finished dealing with an interruption or crisis.

THE NECESSITY OF PLANNING

If you don't know where you are going, you'll end up somewhere else. This trick phrasing reveals more than a little truth. Most people are rather vague about their destinations. They are even more vague about how they expect to reach those destinations. This is particularly true if the destination is a career goal or a financial objective.

Many people will plan a vacation elaborately. They will know where they are going, when they will leave, how they will travel, when they will arrive, how long they will stay, and how they will get back home. These same people may not have spent as much as an afternoon selecting a career goal or planning for financial security in retirement. They trust to fate or to their responsiveness to evolving situations. However, neither fate nor responsiveness is adequate to the task.

To some people planning is an overwhelming or frightening task best left to the "experts." The idea of planning even the most modest project immobilizes them. But planning does not need to be intimidating. Effective planning has little to do with educational level, money, or professional status. Effective planning is much more closely related to having a burning desire to accomplish a particular objective and a willingness to pay attention to the proper sequencing of necessary activities. One of the best planners we know barely graduated from high school. Yet she runs a successful flower shop, rears three teenage children with a lovingly firm hand, and is very active in community affairs. She manages to do all this calmly and pleasantly. Without planning she would have fewer accomplishments and a higher stress level.

THE LINK BETWEEN GOALS AND ACTION

Planning breathes life into goals. While goals have the ability to inspire and motivate action, that action may not necessarily produce the desired accomplishments. Actions must be focused to produce the results desired. Planning directs and focuses actions. Planning transforms mere effort into results. A good plan promotes and guides the efficient and timely use of resources. The same amount of energy may be expended with or without a plan. However, far more will be accomplished if the energy is channeled by a plan.

Work not directed by a plan often produces inconsistent results. All of us face the dilemma of having more demands made on our time than we can possibly fulfill. We could spend a full day doing things whch are our legitimate responsibility, but still neglect our most important responsibilities. Planning ensures that most of your time is devoted to your more important responsibilities.

We are also the victims of Parkinson's law more often than we would like to admit. C. Northcote Parkinson devised a series of interesting "laws" designed to explain why things do not go as well as we often hope they will. Parkinson's law states that "activity will expand to fill the time available." The major implication of Parkinson's law is that how busy you are bears little relationship to your actual level of accomplishment. Structuring activities by planning and scheduling tends to hold Parkinson's law at bay. Planning encourages you to create a series of self-imposed deadlines. Scheduling structures activities in a way that promotes meeting the deadlines.

Effective planning has four important features. If any of these four factors is missing, then you are likely to fall short of the potential inherent in planning. The key ingredients in planning are:

1. Plans should be based on goals. The goals should be clearly defined, attainable, and "owned" by you.
2. Your daily, weekly, and monthly goals should be integrated with your longer-term goals.
3. Your planning activity should be on a schedule. You should plan whether you feel like it or not. You should do your planning at a set time.
4. Your plan should be realistic. Some people get carried away when they first begin to plan and devise a weekly plan that would take four people two weeks to accomplish.

Effective planning starts with identifying the desired end results. The end results can be anything from the installation of a new computer system to a vacation in London. Before you begin planning, you need to have a very detailed and specific picture of the results you want to achieve. If the goal is the installation of a new computer system, then it is important to specify what the new computer should be able to do, how much you are willing to pay for the system, and when you want the installation to be complete. The most complete the picture, the better the plan you can devise.

When you have a detailed and concrete image of your goal, you can begin to identify the resources it will take to accomplish the task. You can begin to estimate the amount of money, time, and resources it will take to get the job done. Perhaps the most critical decision is establishing a deadline. A deadline allows you to start scheduling activities, and a schedule transforms distant goals into today's manageable tasks.

DEVELOPING A SCHEDULE

You probably schedule many of your activities already. Next week's dental appointment is probably on your calendar. You may have an appointment to make a proposal to a customer, or you may have a series of meetings planned to introduce your organization's employees to the new fringe benefit plan. In simplified form these are all part of your schedule. Now you need to apply a few principles to your scheduling practices to multiply the power of scheduling.

Scheduling Principle 1: Expect the unexpected.

The world is an unpredictable place. Emergencies arise; crises develop. An unyieldingly rigid schedule will cause more problems than it will solve. While a schedule is necessary to focus your attention and keep you on track, your schedule should not be so rigid that you are unable to react immediately to unforeseen events. As a general rule, add between 20 percent and 40 percent to the estimated time you think an activity will take. This should give you enough leeway to react to serious unanticipated problems while focusing most of your attention on scheduled priorities.

Scheduling Principle 2: Cushion your schedule.

The most common interruptions will continue to plague you no matter how effectively you manage your time. Phone calls, drop-in visitors, commuting time between appointments, and so on will still be problems no matter what preventative measures you take. Realize that not every moment can or should be put to good account. Build a small cushion into your schedule. You will finish the day less harried, and those who interact with you will not feel neglected or short-changed when they seek your attention.

Scheduling Principle 3: Schedule your most vital
activities when you are at your physical and
mental peak.

As is the case with everyone, you have a two- to four-hour
block of time during the day when you operate at peak efficiency. Your concentration is keen, your creative powers are
more acute, and your ability to do more than one thing at a time
is sharper. Pinpoint this time and schedule your most important
activities within this block of time.

Scheduling Principle 4: Concentrate on the early part
of your day.

Start your day early. Many executives begin their day as
early as 6 A.M. because they know they will have up to two hours
of uninterrupted time. An amazing amount of work can be accomplished if you can concentrate on one task at a time. Getting
a solid accomplishment under your belt early in the morning
gives you a psychological boost that can keep you motivated all
day.

Scheduling Principle 5: Do high-priority things first.

When preparing your schedule, fill in your essential tasks
first and work everything else in around them. If your schedule
gets disrupted, it is likely that the high-priority items will suffer
less.

Scheduling Principle 6: Reserve large blocks of time
for important activities.

Some tasks are difficult or impossible to do if only small
blocks of time are devoted to them. This is especially true when
several people need to reach an agreement about a complex issue. A collective bargaining agreement cannot be achieved if
both sides devote only a few minutes a day to the task. Many
times it is useful to try to finish a task in one sitting. With some
jobs, the difficulty of becoming reacquainted with the problem
keeps you from making significant progress in small blocks of
time. When the momentum is interrupted, efficiency decreases.

Scheduling Principle 7: Schedule similar
activities together.

You can accomplish more if jobs that require basically the
same activities are lumped together. Going through the mail is
such a task. You collect things you need to answer the mail in
one place and process all the day's mail at the same time.

PUTTING IT ALL TOGETHER

The importance of goal setting is widely recognized. Less widely
recognized is the importance of planning and scheduling to turning goals into daily action. If you integrate long-term and short-
term goals, establish plans related to those goals, and develop
realistic schedules, you will multiply your effectiveness several
fold.

CHAPTER 13

Developing and Maintaining Self-confidence

The high-impact time manager is in the business of making events happen. Situations are to be mastered and shaped, not endured. The high-impact time manager has what the behavioral scientist calls an internal locus of control. In more common terms, we would say effective time managers know their own minds and make their own decisions. Beyond that, they have the power that comes from self-confidence.

THE POWER OF SELF-CONFIDENCE

The world can be a tough and unforgiving place. Success is not guaranteed. In the richest country in the world, there are people without homes. There are people who are hungry. These are people overwhelmed by their circumstances, and they deserve our compassion and our assistance.

In contrast, there are people who have faced severe obstacles and triumphed. While there are many reasons why some people master circumstances and others do not, those who beat the odds seem to possess self-confidence in abundance. The self-confident person does not accept the current situation as permanent. The self-confident person expects the situation to change for the better and is absolutely certain that better times are ahead.

When deciding on a course of action, self-confident people seem to ignore the odds. They do not decide whether to proceed by taking a poll. They have very little respect for conventional wisdom or prudence founded on pessimism. They are unimpressed by arguments that assert that a thing should not be done simply because it hasn't been done before. Those with abundant self-confidence also are disdainful of claims about what is and is not possible.

The self-confident person knows some important secrets that enable them to master circumstances and claim accomplishments that elude the timid and unsure. Act on the four secrets of self-confidence, and you will be amazed at the impact you will have on the world around you.

Secret 1: The world yields to hard work.

Hard work is an old-fashioned virtue. The United States was transformed from a wilderness into a great industrial power based on this secret. The nineteenth century was characterized by rapid progress in all areas of the economic life of America. A continent was spanned, a bloody Civil War was fought, major industries were developed. All these things happened with a population that was largely uneducated. Their secret was the willingness to work hard.

Much of the hard work was done by immigrants who regarded the United States as a wonderful opportunity for political freedom and economic prosperity. They seized that opportunity with a vengeance and made their dreams a reality. During the twentieth century we see plenty of evidence that hard work continues to pay off. However, today's cultural norms do not clearly recognize the virtue of hard work. Popular culture is more likely to endorse the pleasure principle, the quick buck, and the shortcut.

Self-confident high achievers realize the value of hard work regardless of whether or not it is in vogue. Sustained effort is simply the price that must be paid to shape events. Self-confident people disregard the odds because they know the oddsmakers underestimate their willingness to work hard. Hard work is an inelegant, brute force means of accomplishing things, but we should never forget how well it works. Sometimes it is the only thing that works.

Secret 2: The world yields to applied intelligence.

As we approach the twenty-first century, it is becoming more and more apparent that most people are employed as information workers. These are jobs that require a person to manage data and work with information rather than things. That such jobs require intelligence goes without saying.

The world is full of problems begging for intelligent solutions. Our list would include stable economies, the challenges of global competitors, poverty, war, and ecological stability. You no doubt have your own list of problems worthy of solution.

It's a good bet that the solutions to most of the problems on both our list and your list will come from invention, innovation, and creativity. The world pays a premium for intelligent problem solving. Self-confident people apply their intelligence in an optimistic manner, expecting to find solutions to the problems they pose for themselves.

Secret 3: The world yields to people who know what they want.

It's easy to drift through life, and many people take this approach. They respond to circumstances, making adjustments that reduce risk and minimize pain. They seek quick fixes, immediate gratification, and small comforts. They dream no impossible dreams, make no serious efforts, and propose no grand schemes. Life is approached tentatively, as if one shouldn't expect too much of life. If resistance is encountered along one path, the drifter abandons that course and tries another, easier road. The drifter willingly compromises, seeking to avoid conflict and confrontation. This approach yields only small successes and small failures.

The self-confident person takes a different approach, believing that virtually anything is possible if one is willing to pay the price. Self-confident people approach goals with a definiteness of purpose. There is no tentativeness here. They know what they want and fully *expect* to get it. They expect resistance along the path to any worthwhile goal. The self-confident person faces the resistance and pushes ahead. Conflict and confrontation are embraced. In fact, they are regarded as problem-solving tools which will eventually assist in reaching the desired goal.

Drifters make way for self-confident people. Unsure of the correct course of action, tentative about their own goals, the drifters are more than accommodating when dealing with people who definitely know what they want. In fact, drifters frequently become followers and allies of self-confident people because they are attracted to the latter's clarity of purpose.

Secret 4: Grand visions and audacity attract allies.

Grand visions precede great accomplishments. Why do grand visions and audacious actions create allies? People become allies because there is a strong need to transcend the routine and established. We crave novel experiences and are attracted by the boldness of charismatic leaders.

Lee Iaccoca's provides a useful example of the power of grand visions and audacious action. Fired after a long career at Ford Motor Company, Iaccoca was offered the presidency of an ailing Chrysler Corporation.

He self-confidently went about turning the company around. His first task was to create a new vision of Chrysler that was inspiring enough to attract the kind of help he would need to achieve a turnaround. His vision consisted of two parts. First, his vision consisted of a Chrysler restored to profitability without the wholesale destruction of American jobs. Second, he envisioned a Chrysler that could compete with the Japanese on style, quality, and price.

The power of this vision was such that Iaccoca was able to attract a talented management team from his former employer, Ford Motor Company, and convince Congress to guarantee loans to finance the restructuring of the company. Not only was the turnaround successful, but Chrysler was able to pay back its guaranteed loans early. Iaccoca, for his part, became one of the best known executives in the country.

BUILDING GREATER SELF-CONFIDENCE

The benefits of behaving self-confidently are evident and appealing. Recognizing the benefits of self-confidence is one thing; acting with self-confidence is another. For most of us, self-confidence is undermined by fear and doubt. We cannot act self-confidently because, in fact, we are *not* self-confident. This dilemma can be overcome by consciously and systematically setting out to build your self-confidence. The following is a step-by-step method for building your self-confidence.

Step 1: Defeat your fears by facing them.

Fear can be healthy and prudent. Fear of death and injury causes us to drive with care and to use our seat belts. Fear of an impoverished old age causes us to establish retirement funds and add to our savings. However, fear can also be unhealthy and lead to self-defeating behavior.

Overwhelming fear paralyzes the mind, causing either inaction or panicky flight. Most of our fears are irrational insofar as the things we fear are not as threatening as we imagine. Such fears include fear of flying, fear of making speeches before groups, fear of making important sales calls, fear of being alone, and fear of the dark.

Irrational fears are best defeated by confrontation. If you have a fear of public speaking, force yourself to face that fear. Examine what it is about speaking in public that intimidates you. Is the fear that you will appear stupid? Do you fear that people will laugh or disagree with you? Knowing specifically what you fear is important for dealing with the fear.

Put yourself on the spot. Volunteer to give a speech to a small, informal group. Pick an audience that is friendly and unintimidating. If your specific fear is that you will appear stupid, spend time in the library researching your topic. A few hours invested this way will virtually guarantee that you will know more about your topic than members of your audience. Whatever your specific fear, take positive action to overcome the problem.

Finally, make the speech. You may find it painful, but your worst nightmare will not come true. You won't die, you won't faint, and the audience will not boo you. In all likelihood, the experience will be much less harrowing than you expect. Reality is seldom a match for your imagination in this regard.

With this experience under your belt, set up a second speech. Perhaps you could give the same speech to a different group. This would allow you to work on any rough spots encountered in your first foray as a public speaker. Continue to put yourself on the spot by volunteering for speeches until you have conquered your fear.

This step-by-step procedure of facing your fears directly

and taking positive actions will enable you to overcome your fear and behave with self-confidence. This approach will work for almost any type of irrational fear.

Step 2: Build your self-confidence by remembering past successes.

We lack self-confidence because of the way we think about our pasts. Painful experiences are etched into the memory. Embarrassing incidents from decades ago can be instantly recalled with as much vividness as if they happened last week. We may even blush at their recalling.

Our failures and embarrassments are not only remembered, but we have a tendency to continue to punish ourselves for them. Forgiving others is easy compared to forgiving ourselves. If we constantly remind ourselves of our weaknesses, faults, shortcomings, and failures, is it any wonder that we lack self-confidence?

The tendency to dwell on the negative aspects of past performance results in unfair comparisons with other people. We tend to contrast our own weakest points to other people's strongest points. We stack our own failures up against other people's success. This is a self-inflicted losing game, and you should stop playing it immediately.

You can call up past successes from your memory just as easily as past failures. Confident people look to the past for reinforcement for positive and optimistic expectations. They dwell on their triumphs and obstacles overcome. They recall how their skills were adequate to the job in the past and take comfort in that when they contemplate difficult assignments to come. They reflect on their capacity for hard work and resourcefulness. The self-confident person uses past successes to nurture the belief that upcoming challenges can be met effectively.

The self-confident person also makes good use of previous defeats and failures. The self-confident person does not regard past failure as evidence of present personal inadequacy. Past failures or defeats are regarded as learning experiences that build skills, understanding, strength. In this fashion, the self-confident person transforms failures into the building blocks of future success.

Step 3: Build an inspiring vision.

Many people lack self-confidence because they are not involved in any undertaking that is inspiring enough to engage their commitment and stimulate their motivation. Small goals and routine tasks do not inspire great efforts. Great dreams and grand visions do. Your greatest disappointments will come from dreaming too small rather than dreaming too large.

The first person you have to inspire is yourself. You cannot tap the enthusiasm and motivation in others unless you have first tapped it in yourself. Your vision needs to be based on values that are important to you. Otherwise, your commitment and motivation are likely to flag when you meet opposition. The importance of an inspiring vision to high achievement is covered in detail in the chapter devoted to goal setting.

Step 4: Capitalize on your uniqueness.

Aspiring novelists are counseled to develop their own styles and voices. People seek out artists who have unique styles. No one takes a singer seriously who merely imitates an already successful performer. The original is always preferred to the copy.

Marketers have long recognized the importance of differentiating one product from another. The more unique a product, the easier it is to market. W. C. Fields with an ordinary voice would have been merely another overweight grouch. Rather than disguise your unique characteristics, you need to capitalize on them.

Concentrating on your unique characteristics will allow you to offer something that few if any other people can match. Your uniqueness is produced by your genetic makeup, your family background, your personality, your specialized training, and your personal experiences. The combination of these factors should provide you with a set of predispositions, talents, interests, and skills possessed by no one else.

Your task is to discover your unique strengths and make maximum use of them. Position yourself to offer your unique capabilities to the world, and you will find the relevant competition diminishes significantly. Find your competitive advantage and make the most of it.

Step 5: Prepare yourself for opportunity.

According to the old saying, opportunity favors the prepared. You prepare for opportunity by deepening your specialized skills and broadening your general skills. While these seem to be contradictory suggestions, they are not.

Most people get their first several jobs based on their specialized skills. People are hired because they can program a computer, repair an automatic transmission, search a database, or assist a customer who needs to buy a particular product. The skills it takes to obtain the job initially are rudimentary. In most cases, it takes years to master the subtleties of any job. Whatever your occupation, continued self-education will increase your value and prepare you to seize opportunity when it presents itself.

You should work to broaden your skills as well. While you should learn your craft or profession thoroughly, you should develop yourself more broadly. Learn about your organization as a whole. Become familiar with the jobs of people who interact with you. Learn about their strengths and their problems. Practice viewing the world from their perspective. If you are an accountant, broaden your skills by learning about manufacturing techniques and marketing strategies. Whatever your occupation, improve your communication skills.

Preparing yourself in this way will make it possible for you to perceive opportunities where others only see problems. When you can see problems from more than one perspective, you become a better problem solver.

Step 6: Expect great things to happen.

Approach the world with a positive expectancy. You will follow up on opportunities only if you can see what might be instead of just what is. Where one person sees dirty cars, another sees an opportunity for a new car wash. Where one person sees unemployment, another sees an opportunity for a trade school. Where one person sees a bankrupt business, another sees the potential for a thriving enterprise. The difference is in the perspective and the expectations.

Charles Tandy encountered a struggling chain of electronics retail stores in the late 1950s. The company had a negative net worth, every store was losing money, and bankruptcy was imminent. But Tandy perceived an opportunity and bought the troubled chain for $5,000 out of pocket. Expecting great things, Tandy aggressively restructured the product line, hired additional people, and started opening new stores. Over the next 20 years, he turned Radio Shack into the nation's largest chain of electronics retailers.

Tandy had the typical attitude of a self-confident person. He was convinced that great things were going to happen when he got involved in Radio Shack. This expectancy allowed him to have the courage to begin opening new stores before the established stores in the chain had become profitable.

Step 6: Leverage your actions by involving other people in your projects.

Self-confident people are not afraid to swim against the tide or to stand up against majority opinion when they believe that they are right. However, they are not loners. They believe so strongly in their goals that they look for ways to accelerate the accomplishment of those goals.

One of the best ways to accelerate the achievement of goals is to get other people involved. A person working alone has only a limited impact. A general without an army, even a Napoleon, can accomplish very little. Leaders achieve greatness by inspiring others to join their causes. Self-confident people in all walks of life understand the importance of sharing their dreams and involving others in their accomplishments.

MASTERING TOUGH SITUATIONS

It's easy to have self-confidence when everything is going well. Under these circumstances, there is no conflict between your positive, optimistic image of yourself and the world's apparent opinion of you. The test of your self-confidence comes when you face tough situations.

When you are broke and disgraced, self-confidence is difficult. When you have made a fool of yourself, behaving with self-confidence is a challenge. When you have been proven wrong repeatedly, having confidence in your own opinions is difficult. Yet these are precisely the circumstances in which self-confidence pays its greatest dividends. Self-confidence can survive tough times if it is supported by three things

- Willpower
- Faith
- Persistence

When Harlan Sanders was 65 years old, a new highway by-passed his successful restaurant and bankrupted him. Instead of retiring, Sanders used his Social Security check to pay expenses as he went on the road to sell his secret recipe for fried chicken. He was confident that other restaurant owners would want his recipe for chicken that was finger lickin' good. Eventually, his self-confident efforts established the Kentucky Fried Chicken franchise chain and secured his own fortune.

Harlan Sanders is a testimony to the importance of willpower. In spite of the odds, he *willed* his new business and his new fortune into being. He simply refused to be defeated.

A teenager's faith in a dream allowed him to create a whole new industry in less than five years. Steven Jobs created the Apple Computer company and the microcomputer industry in his mind before his first computer was even functional. He dreamed of changing the shape of computing, placing the power of computers into the hands of everyone. He dreamed of a computer that would be inexpensive, attractive, unintimidating, and easy to use.

His faith in his dream allowed him to attract hard-boiled engineers from Hewlett-Packard at reduced salaries. He was able to convince suppliers to take a chance on a kid not yet 20 years old. He convinced retailers that there would be a large consumer market for a brand-new product. Before Apple Computer, only hobbyists with the skills to assemble electronic kits owned their own personal computers. Today millions of children are growing up in homes where they learn to use the personal computer before they can read.

This transformation was created by the initial faith one young man had in his vision. Faith was the power that transmuted Steven Jobs's ideas into reality.

Our story about persistence is old and well known. When R. U. Darby was a young man, he and an uncle went prospecting for gold. They discovered a vein, staked a claim, and proceeded to get down to the serious business of getting the ore out of the mine. All went well at first, but a curious thing happened. The vein disappeared. They continued to drill without success and finally gave up in disgust.

The man who bought the claim from them for a few hundred dollars called in a mining engineer. He advised them to keep drilling, speculating that the vein would reappear. Three feet deeper, the new owner struck gold. A little more persistence and Mr. Darby and his uncle would have been millionaires.

SUMMARY

Self-confident people are powerful. They shape fate instead of fall victim to it. Fully aware that ideas give birth to reality, they dream grand dreams and envision great accomplishments. Current reality is of less concern to them than is the vision they expect to create through hard work, intelligence, and resourcefulness.

Self-confidence is especially important in adversity. During tough times self-confidence frequently makes the difference between success and failure. The winners know how to create, nurture, build, and sustain their self-confidence. In tough times, they employ willpower, faith, and persistence to maintain their self-confidence.

Index